Texas Tavern

MERCER UNIVERSITY PRESS

Endowed by

TOM WATSON BROWN
and
THE WATSON-BROWN FOUNDATION, INC.

"Restaurants nurture people and sustain communities. Each day since 1930, the Texas Tavern has proved that theorem. This story of service, stewardship, and cold buttermilk reminds us all of the power and promise of the common table."

John T Edge

author of *The Potlikker Papers: A Food History of the Modern South*

"The Cheesy Western and a Bowl With have finally gotten what they have long-deserved . . . their own book! Shari Dragovich gives us all the lore that is one part biography, two parts food—with a generous mix of local history and seasoned with delicious anecdotes from some who have dined at the Millionaires Club. Dragovich's timely work about a timeless institution and the family behind it all is literary soul food for those of us who cherish food heritage and greasy spoon hospitality."

Nelson Harris

historian and former Mayor of Roanoke, Virginia

"If the ten stools at Texas Tavern could talk they would tell the story of America, and Shari Dragovich has done an excellent job at making those stools talk. She has captured a vital piece of the gastronomic fabric of America by reminding us all that even the under-appreciated hamburger has a place in history. I for one selfishly applaud the continued vitality of Texas Tavern because it means I'll always be able to sit at one of those famous stools, anytime of the day or night, and enjoy my beloved Triple Meat Cheesy, hold the Sissy Sauce."

George Motz

author of *Hamburger America* and host of *Burger Scholar Sessions*

MUP/ P614

978-0-88146-760-4

Published by Mercer University Press
1501 Mercer University Drive
Macon, Georgia 31207

FIRST EDITION

9 8 7 6 5 4 3 2 1

Books published by Mercer University Press are printed on acid-free paper
that meets the requirements of the American National Standard for Information Sciences—
Permanence of Paper for Printed Library Materials.

Book design by Burt&Burt
Text set in Cambria and Clarendon
Printed in Canada

Cataloging-in-Publication Data is available from the Library of Congress

Texas Tavern

Four Generations of the Millionaires Club

SHARI L. DRAGOVICH

MERCER UNIVERSITY PRESS

Macon, Georgia | 2020

*For Tony,
the Bullingtons,
and Roanokers.*

Thank you.

*"This series explores the central and profound role
that food and foodways play in understanding the South's past,
its present, and its future. Through a broad variety of academic disciplines,
the series examines the region's culinary history, celebrates the glories
of the Southern table, and analyzes the many influences that
come together to define Southern food."*

Fred W. Sauceman
Series Editor

In the Series

Mary Bohlen's Heritage Cooking: Inspired by Rebecca Boone
Mary Bohlen

The Proffitts of Ridgewood: An Appalachian Family's Life in Barbecue
Fred W. Sauceman

Cook & Tell: Recipes and Stories from Southern Kitchens
Johnathon Scott Barrett, ed.

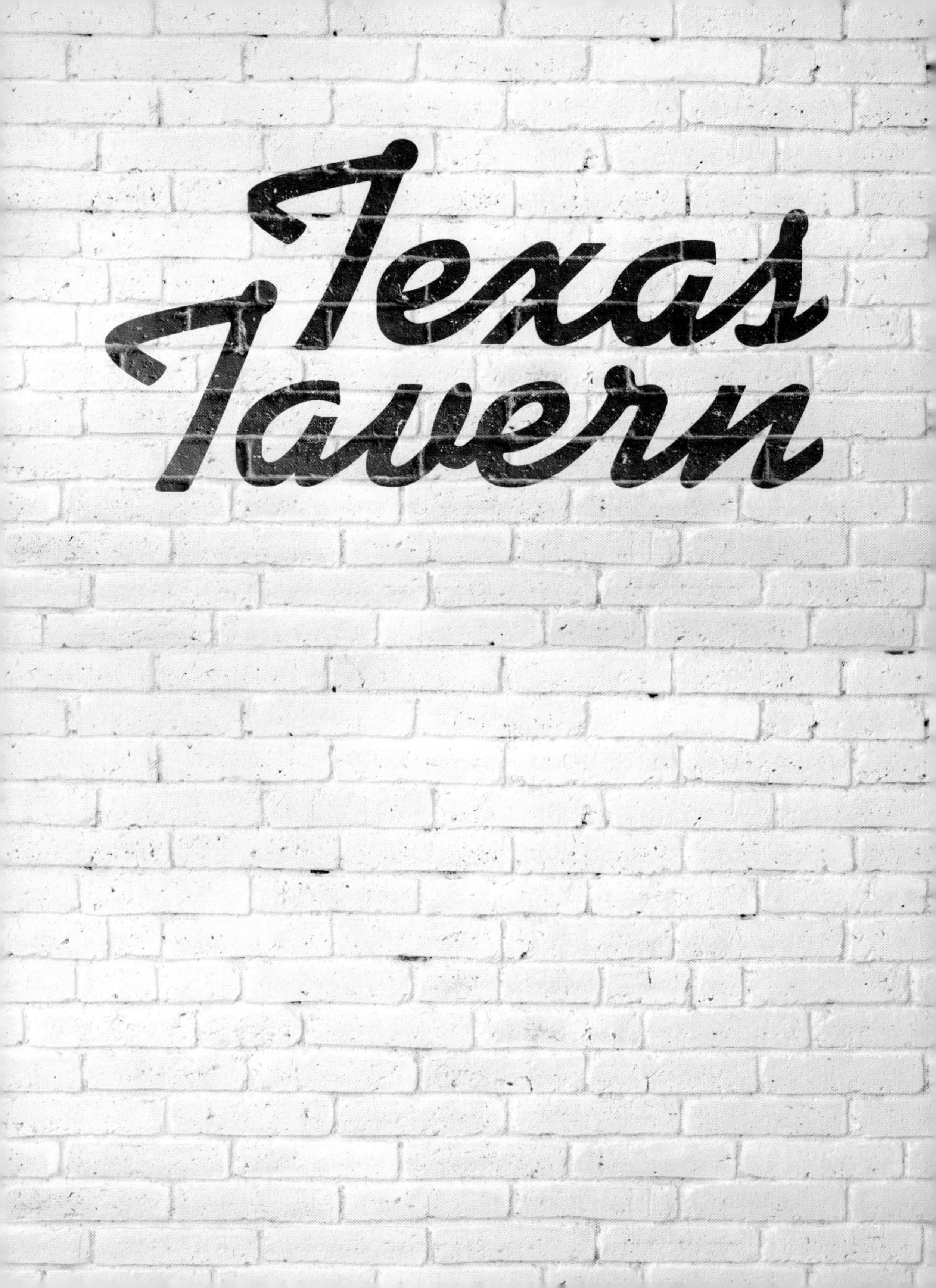
Texas
Tavern

The ten counter stools at the Texas Tavern in Roanoke, Virginia, are sacred spaces. Diners have been occupying them since 1930. That year, Isaac Newton "Nick" Bullington, once a nomadic circus promoter from the Midwest, settled amid the Blue Ridge Mountains of Virginia and never left. Nor did his family. The Texas Tavern is now in the fourth generation of Bullington family ownership.

Matt Bullington, Nick's great-grandson, pondered other careers and even considered law school, but he had the good sense to devote his life to the preservation of the family business. Realizing that his great-grandfather started the Tavern during one of the most difficult times in American history—as the Great Depression was deepening—Matt has always felt a profound responsibility to keep it going through pure hard work. Except for a few hours at Christmas, The Texas Tavern never closes.

Millions of customers, from governors to bricklayers, parolees to parish priests, have rested their elbows on the original stainless steel counter, in anticipation of a quirky burger called the Cheesy Western, dressed with cabbage relish, and a bowl of "e" on the end chile, from a recipe Nick Bullington finagled from a cook at the Palace Hotel in San Antonio, Texas, in the 1920s.

That's about the only Texas connection there is at the Tavern, and, despite the name, not a drop of alcohol is sold. A drink of choice here is buttermilk.

A restaurant that has been in operation this long, on the same spot, and in the hands of the same family, is a precious rarity in America. The stories that have been passed up and down that ten-seat counter are as dear to the citizens of Roanoke as the food. Customers tell of eating at The Texas Tavern before going off to World War II. Of being hidden in the back room to escape a school's truant officer. And of having their meals interrupted by Roanoke firefighters, who insisted that it might be a good idea for diners to abandon their bowls of chile, at least long enough for the blaze in the back of the restaurant to be extinguished.

Those stories and that long history, now exceeding ninety years, needed to be documented in book form. And Shari Dragovich was the perfect person to do it. Not only did Shari spend countless hours interviewing members of the Bullington family, she also got behind the counter, even after midnight, when, as Matt says, "The fun begins." Shari learned the art and architecture of the Cheesy Western, and she can now make chile with the best of the countermen.

Like the Tavern itself, this book that Shari has created connects food and memory in a deeply respectful way. As she so clearly and lovingly proves, the Texas Tavern is an American treasure.

Fred Sauceman
Series Editor

MORE THAN A RESTAURANT

When I was a child, my family would eat lunch out most Sundays after church. There weren't many choices in the small Illinois farming community where I grew up. There was the Crossroads Truck Stop about a mile outside of town, at the intersection of Old Route 66 and State Route 138. Ten miles up the road, in Litchfield, were the old Ariston Cafe or Maverick Steak House, one of those all-you-can-eat chain buffet places considered "up-and-coming" in the 1980s. When I was very small there was also an old Howard Johnson operating under independent owners and by a different name. They served chocolate milk in chilled, cow-shaped glass mugs. I was allowed one glass per visit, making it my favorite restaurant by far. But it was shuttered by the time I'd turned eight years old.

Most of the time my family dined at the Crossroads. It was closest to our home and the most affordable. I always ordered the same thing: a plain cheese sandwich with applesauce and green beans. The sandwich was made with white Wonder Bread and two slices of Kraft American cheese. The green beans were from a can and served swimming in their salty canning juices. The applesauce was the smoothest, most uniform stuff I'd ever eaten outside of Jell-O or pudding, neither of which I was allowed on a regular basis. These food products were exotic to me, as they were not a part of my daily diet. I was raised on a medium-sized hog farm. My father, besides raising hogs, farmed cash crops: corn, wheat, and soybeans. My mother kept a large garden of the likes I've rarely seen outside those historic living museums I enjoy visiting today. She canned and froze and kept our basement cellar stocked with the literal fruits and vegetables of her labor. Always our freezers were full of pork and other local farmers' meats. To a kid whose daily bread was made almost daily, the food at Crossroads was exciting.

I have fond memories of our family's meals at Crossroads. But I would never claim the Crossroads itself was a beloved place in my community. It wasn't a place my friends and I wanted to frequent as teenagers. I would have been offended if my boyfriend, who is now my husband, had taken me to Crossroads on a date. I did go back once with my toddling son—decades ago. It was another post-church outing with my folks. It was also one of those moments you realize how you remembered a place is far removed from reality. Shortly after that visit, Crossroads shut down.

✪ ✪ ✪ ✪ ✪ ✪ ✪ ✪ ✪ ✪ ✪ ✪ ✪ ✪ ✪

What makes a restaurant more than a restaurant? How does a food place transcend its expressed function and turn into an institution? How does it become a cultural mooring, even an icon: a treasured food endeavor beloved by its members and looked to as the embodiment of their place? I wonder these things. I especially wonder them as a native Midwesterner, living in and fully embracing the South as home.

Twelve years ago, when I first moved south of the Mason-Dixon line, I recognized something important about being a Southerner. In the South, folks and food and place abide together in a holy relationship as One. In many ways, I can identify with the deep and soulful way Southerners connect with one another and their place through food. Growing up I was nourished directly by the land on which I was raised. I even had a part in the labor of that land. Likewise, I grew up with the modeling and practice of fellowship around shared meals. At home around the family dinner table and also in our community. Midwesterners have their fair share of church picnics, potlucks, and ice cream socials, too.

However, there are things about Southerners and their food culture that puzzle me. For example, why must the debate surrounding barbecue be so heated? And what is this gift possessed by Southern writers for turning topics like sweet tea and pickled beets into treatises on life?

But, what fuels my Southern food wonderings the most—indeed, what has captured my heart for the South—is this: *Food*, says the Southerner, *is story*. And not just any story. Food tells the best kind of story. It's a story steeped in the specifics of time and place. It is generational in its telling and is deeply personal. Yet it is expressed in a way that transcends itself. The food story has the power to illuminate truth and light a good way forward. Finally, like every beautiful and worthy story, the story food tells culminates in communion and fullness for its membership.

Enter here the story of the Texas Tavern: a ten-stool hamburger and hot dog joint that truly is an institution within its community and cultural mooring for society at large. All my questions and wonderings above led me to the Texas Tavern. In turn, the Texas Tavern graciously opened itself to me and offered up its answers. And it did so in that most distinguished of Southern ways, by telling me its story. This is the driving force behind *Texas Tavern: Four Generations of the Millionaires Club*.

But first, let me introduce you to Roanoke, the place both the Texas Tavern and I call home.

✪ ✪ ✪ ✪ ✪ ✪ ✪ ✪ ✪ ✪ ✪ ✪ ✪ ✪ ✪ ✪

Roanoke is nestled between folds of the Southern Appalachian Mountains of southwest Virginia. It lies in a valley—a gap where mountains otherwise bunch and roll, one into another. The valley itself is an oblong space about twenty miles long and ten miles at its widest point, tapering quickly to around five miles on the ends. It sits in the middle of two other valleys: the New River to the southwest, and the famous Shenandoah to the northeast. In official language, Roanoke Valley is

Roanoke photographed from the same vantage point in 1882 (above) and 1902 (below).
(Courtesy of Virginia Room, Roanoke Public Libraries)

part of the Ridge and Valley Province of Virginia. But most folks know the mountains around Roanoke as the Blue Ridge.

Driving along Interstate 81, you'd be inclined to think Roanoke amounts to a series of truck stops, food chains, and single-night hotel stays—a town for the weary traveler, but not much else. You would be wrong to think that today. But a passing-through point is exactly how Roanoke began.

According to *The History of Roanoke City*, written by E. B. Jacobs in 1912, Roanoke grew out of a crossroads. Long before it was settled by European immigrants, Roanoke was a stop along the "Great Path," a Native American route running northeast-southwest in the most direct way possible through the Appalachian Range. The Great Path began as a pathway whereby northern and southern tribes communicated with one another. During the colonial era, it became part of the Great Wagon Road, the most heavily traveled road of the eighteenth century.

In the Roanoke Valley—in the area now known as Old Gainsboro—the Great Path broke off in different directions. One path headed eastward. The other took a more southerly route toward the Carolinas. The valley also contained two water features: the Roanoke River cutting through it, and a natural spring, later named Crystal Spring. These made the Roanoke Valley an appealing camping ground for Indians, and later a popular outpost for pioneers and settlers on their way to the lands of the Blue Ridge and beyond. The outpost was called "Big Lick" because of the large salt marsh located near the natural spring, attracting deer and other animals to it by droves.

While Roanoke is known today for its prominence in the railroad industry, it was tobacco that initiated the first efforts at settlement. Big Lick incorporated as a town in 1874. In its earliest years as a town, Big Lick boasted five tobacco factories and three tobacco warehouses. Along with this came all the supporting businesses needed for a town to thrive: plaster and flour mill, two blacksmiths, a harness manufacturer, one plow and wagon manufacturer, seven dry goods stores, two photography studios, three churches, and three saloons. Big Lick grew steadily under these conditions, making it an attractive location to industries to begin or expand their operations.

In 1881, Frederick J. Kimball, president of the Shenandoah Valley Railroad, chose Big Lick to be a connecting point with the larger Norfolk & Western Railroad. Seeing their town's bright future, the citizens of Big Lick pulled together and worked to secure the funds for improving roadways and other infrastructure necessary for making their town "railroad industry" ready. One of their tasks included renaming Big Lick. Citizens agreed a great railroad town needed a distinguished name. Townspeople brought forth two contenders: "Roanoke," after the river, and "Kimball," after Shenandoah Railroad's president. When asked, Mr. Kimball declined the honor. On February 3, 1882, Big Lick became Roanoke. By 1912, Roanoke had incorporated as a city. It also had an official history written of its stunning progress, and was on a trajectory of roaring growth decades into the twentieth century.

This was the state of Roanoke when founder and first-generation owner of the Texas Tavern Nick Bullington discovered it.

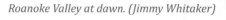

Roanoke Valley at dawn. (Jimmy Whitaker)

Texas Tavern

NICK BULLINGTON

Within the soul of America is freedom of mind and spirit in man. Here alone are the open windows through which pours the sunlight of the human spirit. Here alone is human dignity not a dream but an accomplishment. Perhaps it is not perfect, but it is more full in realization here than any other place in the world.

PRESIDENT HERBERT HOOVER

1ST GEN

Isaac Newton Bullington, first generation Texas Tavern owner.

Imagine it's 1930, in the middle of winter. Across the nation, Americans are facing month five of a severe economic downturn. Work is becoming increasingly harder to find, especially the factory work America's immigrants have become reliant upon for establishing new lives. The agricultural markets are already strained from Dust Bowl conditions. Now, with the markets trapped beneath their own collapse, farmers wonder how they'll survive the double whammy of terrible weather and a terrible market. An invisible, heavy noose continues to tighten around the country's neck as months pass and jobs elude large segments of the population. What's worse, there seems no end to it. These are not the days for starting new business ventures.

Except, that's exactly what Nick Bullington—an Indiana-born-and-raised businessman with an adventurous soul and penchant toward the ironic—does. Instead of seeing America's era of depression as a time to hole up and make do, Nick decides he'd like to open himself a small ten-seat, quick-bite chili, hamburger, and hot dog joint. He's seen similar places pop up around the Midwest. They are turning a profit and even expanding their reach across the country. So, with little more than a chili recipe he's procured in San Antonio and his belief in America's growing fascination with this newfangled "fast food" eatery concept, Nick shucks Depression odds and opens his new place. He names it the Texas Tavern. He even chooses the most unlucky number on the calendar on which to open: February 13, 1930.

One might wonder if there was something whimsical or progressive about Nick's childhood and the places he was raised that inspired his adventures and wanderings as an adult. There was not.

Isaac Newton "Nick" Bullington was born September 7, 1877, in Saint Bernice, Indiana, called Jamestown at the time of Nick's birth. His parents, Leander "Lee" Bullington and Margaret Swan, were both native to the Hoosier state. Nick was one of six children born to Lee and Margaret. The couple lost a baby boy at birth, and a daughter, Alice Aline, died at age seven. The other four children lived into adulthood. Nick was number three in that lineup. He was named after his paternal grandfather, who spent his life as a minister of the New Light Church in Orange County, Indiana.

Saint Bernice was—and still is—a small country village located in the far central-western part of Indiana, a stone's throw from the Illinois border. Nick's father, Lee, ran a general store and pharmacy. He was active in the civic life of his community as a member of the Freemasons, a membership maintained through three generations of Bullingtons. Nick's mother, Margaret, beyond raising children and supporting her husband's work, was an active member in the community.

In the mid-1880s, likely around the time Nick was ten years old, the family moved to Clinton, Indiana, ten miles southeast of Saint Bernice, after Margaret inherited money from her father's estate. Clinton would have felt like a booming metropolis for the Bullington family. At that time, it was a popular destination for many immigrant populations, especially northern Italians, Austrians, and Scots, who came to work in the coal mines of the Midwest.

The Bullingtons, however, were not part of the coal mine movement. Leander became a painter after an injury to his right hand made it difficult for him to do the delicate work of handling medicines and running a pharmacy. Margaret immersed herself in the Clinton community as a nursemaid to the town doctor.

Nick grew up watching his parents live and move through the gifts and challenges life handed them. He watched his father overcome personal obstacles and continually adjust to his physical limitations without allowing these limitations to diminish him. He watched his mother—a woman well acquainted with deep grief—move through her own pain of losing children to nursing others through their suffering and loss. He watched both parents live a community-minded life, no matter what hardships they were personally facing.

Though the year is unknown, Nick left Clinton as soon as he had one foot in adulthood. Grover Cleveland was likely president. Urban construction was booming. Telephones were in wide use and moving pictures were a strange curiosity. Radio and air flight were just around the corner. The United States was well ahead of the rest of the world in the age of Industrialization. Indeed, it was a strange new world inviting Nick's participation. Like the rest of America heading into the 1900s, Nick was roiling with ambition and ideas. He was in search of the Big Life.

Nick found his big life under the Big Top: working as an advance man for the Gentry Dog and Pony Show and, later, Ringling Brothers' Circus. While exact dates for Nick's involvement with the "Greatest Show on Earth" are vague, he left clear indicators of his time with Gentry's Dog and Pony Show: dozens of train ticket stubs dating from the years 1898 to 1901, as well as clippings of newspaper articles he wrote promoting the show.

It would have been an exciting time to work for either of these circus acts. Both were on the other side of rapid growth from small Midwestern, animal-drawn caravan acts to nationwide train-traveling show sensations. As an advance man, Nick traveled across the country via railway in his own travel car, setting up contracts a year ahead of the circus's scheduled appearance.

Train stubs Nick Bullington saved from his travels as advance man for the Gentry Dog and Pony Show.

Nick's time as advance man for the Gentry Dog and Pony Show was during the show's rapid trajectory upward. Like Nick, the show had humble beginnings and Indiana roots. By the time Nick Bullington joined the business, there were four shows, each covering its own region of the country. Nick's traveling work concentrated primarily in the South and East with some Midwest travel, too.

There is less physical evidence of Nick's time with Ringling Bros. Circus. However, it is this famous circus that's been passed down through the Bullington generations as the one with which Nick was primarily connected. In whatever ways Nick was connected with Ringling Bros., one thing is clear: America's circus acts and Nick Bullington were coming of age together.

✪ ✪ ✪ ✪ ✪ ✪ ✪ ✪ ✪ ✪ ✪ ✪ ✪ ✪ ✪

In 1902, right after his stint with the Gentry Dog and Pony Show, Nick married Katherine "Cassie" Wise, from Huntington, West Virginia. They were both twenty-five. According to a handwritten family account, the couple moved to Pittsburgh, Pennsylvania, for a short time, where Nick worked in advertising and bill pasting. Then it was back to Huntington.

Nick's wanderlust must have quelled for the moment at least. The couple settled in Huntington for a time. A 1910 Huntington census lists one Isaac and Katherine Bullington as actor and actress in a vaudeville theater. The family account confirms the census reporting, stating the couple owned a theater in Huntington, and acted in it as well. Among the fantastic stories told of Nick Bullington, one is that he hired Devil Anse Hatfield, patriarch of the Hatfield clan—from the famous Hatfields and McCoys—to act in his vaudeville plays. He paid the man in moonshine.

On April 8, 1911, Cassie gave birth to their only child, James Gladstone Bullington. Details of Nick's life become murky after his son's birth. There are the stories that have been handed down through the generations, the primary one being Nick's work with Ringling Bros.

From boxes of old files, letters, and other papers stored in the Bullingtons' basement, there's evidence of Nick owning a traveling circus in South America. This he likely did as a side hustle and on the sly while working for Ringling Bros. He also owned a mattress factory and fertilizer factory. When he was in his mid-thirties, Nick bought the McBeth Building at the corner of Mulberry and Main Street in his hometown of Clinton. It was one of the "most desirable business buildings downtown," according to an old Clinton newspaper clipping. Nick was also active in his support of the troops during the Great War. He offered his binoculars to the war effort in World War I. These were returned to him after the war along with a thank you note written by FDR, who was Assistant Secretary of the Navy, at the time. And then there was the farmland Nick owned in Paris, Illinois, less than twenty miles from Clinton, Indiana.

This was the kind of man Nick Bullington was. His eyes were forever fixed on progress. He was always looking for ways to find and then implement his next idea. This was a man who kept the *Little Golden Business Books* in his back pocket, owned copies of the *Efficient Waiter* and *Practical and Profitable Chinese Recipes*, and saved an advertisement clipping for the Missouri Egg Cooler. Nick was the consummate collector—not of things, necessarily, but of ideas connected with those things. It's clear from the items he saved, Nick Bullington was a man who believed in the potential power of small notions.

It was precisely a small thing—as small as a recipe card even—that led to the eventual icon now called the Texas Tavern. At a San Anto-

Macinac Island Michigan August 1906

Nick and Katherine Bullington, 1906.

nio hotel during one of his many and mysterious business ventures, Nick discovered a chili like none he'd ever tasted before. The beans, the spices, the onions. It must have been some kind of monumental food experience, for Nick set out to obtain the recipe. Nick used every ounce of his theatric marketing genius to convince the manager of the restaurant to give him the recipe. In that exchange, unbeknownst even to Nick himself, the Texas Tavern was conceived.

As zany as it seems for Nick Bullington to open an eatery in the midst of what is still considered the greatest economic crisis in America's history, opening the Texas Tavern wasn't zany at all. A careful study of American culture in the first several decades of the twentieth century shows Nick had discovered and held fast to the pulse of a new, more homogenous America. In fact, opening the Tavern when he did may be one reason it still thrives more than ninety years later.

Just as today's Information Age is fundamentally changing the shape of our culture and how we live, the Industrial Age did the same at the turn of the twentieth century. Everything from the rise of factories, the continual mass migration of ethnic groups, and new inventions and innovations all connected Americans in new ways. Ethnic lines began to blur. A collective American spirit began to emerge.

Along with the driving movement toward a more blended nation, Americans' eating habits began shifting. Always there had been the basic fare offered in boarding houses and the small eateries found in urban ethnic neighborhoods. And then, after the turn of the century, as the automobile and highway system took hold, eating out became a national pastime.

One way Nick would have recognized and been influenced by America's burgeoning restaurant scene is through his transcontinental travels as an advance man. In the first chapter of his book, *Selling 'em by the Sack, White Castle and the Creation of American Food*, David Gerard Hogan takes readers through a quick but fascinating account of restaurant development in America. It began with the railways. In the 1870s,

George Pullman introduced sleeping and dining cars, fundamentally altering train travel to a more high society experience.

Pullman's innovations became the direct inspiration for the development of the diner: the long, narrow eatery with a counter and bar stools where customers—also called *diners*—were offered a small array of basic food fare served hot, fast, and at reasonable prices. As Hogan describes it, creative but "penniless" entrepreneurs would salvage old Pullman cars and transform them into stationary restaurants. They would often position their diners outside a factory where working class men were hankering for a cheap, filling bite to eat before or after their work shift. Soon diners began popping up in urban neighborhoods across the country. They were usually open twenty-four hours. They served breakfast, lunch, dinner, and snacks. Despite the upper classes snubbing such places, even labeling them "restaurants of ill-repute," the diner flourished.

Another influencer in the dining-out transformation of America was restaurateur Henry Harvey. Shortly after the Pullman car developed, Harvey recognized the need for easy, reliable, and affordable food options for rail passengers. He created a restaurant service offering travelers quality fresh foods, pristine eating conditions, and excellent service at affordable prices. Harvey positioned his eateries at train stations throughout the country. He was meticulous about the quality of foods and service. Passengers knew exactly what to expect and came to depend on Harvey restaurants as a dependable option to expensive dining-car food. His was the first true model of standardized food service in America.

Dining cars, diners, and train station eateries. Like his Little Golden Books on business and saved advertisement clippings, Nick stored away restaurant ideas as instinctively as a squirrel collects and stores its acorns. But, more than any of these influences, it's hard to miss the extreme likeness of Nick's Texas Tavern to the early White Castle restaurant model.

According to Hogan, the first White Castle restaurant wasn't a restaurant at all. It was an old, retrofitted shoeshine stand, refurbished by Walter Anderson, a grill cook in Wichita, Kansas. As legend has it, Anderson came upon the inspiration for his White Castle slider sandwich by accident. One day while working the grill at some quick-bite eatery, Anderson—out of frustration—slammed flat a slow-grilling meatball he was tired of cooking. His new, flat hamburger sandwich became so popular with customers, Anderson decided to set out on his own. In 1916, the first White Castle hamburger stand officially opened.

By 1921, Anderson and his White Castle hamburger stands had grown to include a partner, Billy Ingram, who eventually bought Anderson's share of the company, a real building, and multiple locations in Wichita, Kansas. By 1930—the year Nick Bullington opened Texas Tavern—White Castle restaurants could be found in twelve major cities, including St. Paul-Minneapolis and New York City, with a total of 116 restaurants, spanning a geographic area 1,424 miles east to west.

Looking at pictures of the Texas Tavern and the first White Castle restaurants side by side, they are nearly identical: white walls inside and out, a single counter with stationary stools along it, the grill located directly behind the counter within plain view of the customers, and catchy advertising hung on the walls. Anderson's and Ingram's most important early effort with White Castle was to dispel the long-held notion that chopped beef was low-quality, rancid meat. As such, they adopted bright white as White Castle's color, inside and out. Workers wore white starched uniforms, aprons, and hats. Shiny stainless countertops promoted thoughts of hygiene. They had staunch rules about their meat. Throughout the store they displayed catchy slogans, engaging customers and evangelizing their White Castle message. The efforts of Anderson and Ingram in changing America's mind about ground beef and short-order diners helped pave the way for Nick's own Texas Tavern early successes.

✪ ✪ ✪ ✪ ✪ ✪ ✪ ✪ ✪ ✪ ✪ ✪ ✪ ✪ ✪

How does a man from the Midwest, who's traveled the country and beyond, who had roots—however loosely planted—in Huntington, West Virginia; Clinton, Indiana; and Paris, Illinois; decide on Roanoke, Virginia, as *the* destination for his version of the quick-bite diner? He didn't. At least, not at first. Nick Bullington first opened the Texas Tavern in New Castle, Indiana.

New Castle is located forty-eight miles east of Indianapolis. At the time Nick was opening his new restaurant, New Castle was a fast growing town. According to Census Bureau data, New Castle had a population of 666 at the time of its first census in 1850. By 1900 it had grown to a population of 3,406. In 1920, it was at 14,458. New Castle was a manufacturing center for the production of sheet iron and steel. It was also home to the Maxwell Automobile Factory—the largest automobile manufacturing plant in the world at the time of its construction in the early twentieth century.

With all this considered, New Castle made an excellent choice for opening the Texas Tavern. And so, with his saved chili recipe and his eye on the cutting-edge standardization driving White Castle's success, Nick opened his Texas Tavern in New Castle in 1926.

According to old letters, Nick made a business trip to Indianapolis around the same time as the New Castle Tavern's opening. While dining at a local restaurant there, he met Charles Van Cleve, the restaurant's young manager. Nick was impressed with Van Cleve's dynamic personality and professionalism. The two struck up a conversation. By the time it was over, Nick had offered Van Cleve a job managing his Texas Tavern. Van Cleve accepted Nick's offer and moved to New Castle. Over the course of the next two years, Nick traveled and Van Cleve managed the Texas Tavern. The two men corresponded often through letters, discussing everything from tweaks to the chile recipe—to appease the more mild-loving Midwestern palate—to personal family updates.

New Castle Texas Tavern, Charles Van Cleve behind the counter on right, ca. 1928.

By all known accounts, the Texas Tavern was doing well in its Indiana home surrounded by cornfields and squared-off country roads. And then, in the fall of 1929, everything changed. On October 29, Wall Street crashed under the weight of poorly regulated markets, permitting a glut of overoptimistic loans. A nearly decade-long depression ensued. It was one that—at its lowest point—would leave 15 million Americans without employment and more than half the nation's banks in failure.

Nick understood the Texas Tavern would not thrive in a manufacturing and agricultural community during the severe economic downturn. Among those segments of the population hardest hit during the Depression were farmers and manufacturers of consumer goods, both of which built and sustained New Castle's economy. But rather than give up on the Tavern as a casualty of the times, Nick Bullington looked for a new location for his restaurant. Some place not so hard hit. Some place booming, even.

Enter Roanoke, Virginia.

Nick was familiar with Roanoke. He'd been through town several times during his years as an advance man. He'd seen Roanoke's growth and recognized its potential for his business.

Despite the rest of the country's manufacturing downturn, Roanoke's population and manufacturing growth was going strong. In an April 26, 1930 article, the *Roanoke World News* reported Roanoke City grew from a population of 21,495 in 1900 to 69,096 in 1930. Public school enrollment went from 6,266 in 1910 to 14,805 in 1930. Infant mortality dropped from 131 per 1,000 in 1913 to 86 per 1,000 in 1929. Deaths from tuberculosis were cut in half over the same period. Death rates in Roanoke in 1929 were the lowest they'd been in Roanoke's history.

But most impressive were Roanoke's manufacturing gains. In another statistic-driven article dated April 13, 1930, it was noted that in the year 1909, Roanoke held sixty-two manufacturing establishments with 3,554 wage earners and an annual production of $7,251,000. In 1929, even as the Depression was taking hold, Roanoke boasted 140 manufacturing establishments with 21,000 wage earners and an annual production of $70,000,000. In 1930, Norfolk and Western recorded a 25 percent increase over a twelve-month period in freight tonnage with Roanoke as either the destination or origin point. Bank clearings were at an 8 percent increase and bankruptcies were down from the year prior. Area farmers were the only group to suffer during the severe economic downturn. It was a nationwide dilemma no amount of local manufacturing power could curb. Because of Norfolk and Western's unusual expansion during the Depression, Roanoke earned itself national attention. According to family stories passed down through the Bullington generations, Roanoke was named as one of ten top cities in America for business opportunities. None of this was lost on Nick Bullington.

By all indications, Nick had no plans of moving his Texas Tavern prior to the stock market crash. In a letter written by Van Cleve dated September 13, 1929, there is no mention of a new Tavern in Roanoke. By November, all that had changed.

14

Soon after the stock market crash, Nick traveled to Roanoke. He met with Edgar Thurman, owner of the S. H. Heironimus Department Store building, a Roanoke-based department store with several locations throughout Roanoke and Lynchburg. Thurman owned a tiny parcel of land on Church Avenue, big enough to build a shotgun-style diner, nearly identical to his New Castle design. With $1,200 for building costs and a handshake with Thurman to lease the lot, Nick had a new location for his Texas Tavern. He went back to Indiana and closed his New Castle Tavern. He pulled the parts from it he would take to Roanoke: the back bar, grills, and cooking equipment. He then offered Van Cleve the opportunity to move to Roanoke and run the Tavern in its new mountain south location. Van Cleve considered the opportunity but declined. The two men said their goodbyes and Nick left for Roanoke. He rebuilt the Tavern using cinder blocks and the dismantled back wall. He expanded out from either side of the wall to create a space able to accommodate ten stools, three more than the New Castle Tavern. He painted the inside and out bright white with shiny red trim. He replaced his inside sign that read, "We serve 700, 7 at a time," with a new sign announcing, "We serve 1,000, 10 at a time." Finally, he contacted Kinsey Neon & Sign Company to make him a large neon-lit "EAT" sign in the shape of a curving arrow he hung over the entrance.

After all this was in place, Nick Bullington opened his second-time 'round new eatery, the *Roanoke* Texas Tavern. It was Thursday, February 13, 1930. He chose this date on purpose. It was Nick's way of giving folks hope and showing no matter how unlucky times might be, there's always a way to make a new beginning.

Opposite: Above, Roanoke Texas Tavern, 1930; below, Grand Opening in Roanoke on February 13, 1930, Nick Bullington on far left.

Texas Tavern Chile. (Sam Dean)

THE CHILE THAT STARTED IT ALL

"Cheap chili is spelled with an 'i.' Our chile is spelled with an 'e.'"

Jim Bullington

third-generation Texas Tavern owner

"One of the best things about Tavern chile is that you can't buy it at Walmart. They are waiting for it to be manufactured in China, which will never happen."

Dan Casey

from his eighty-first-anniversary Texas Tavern column

✪ ✪ ✪ ✪ ✪ ✪ ✪ ✪ ✪ ✪ ✪ ✪ ✪ ✪ ✪

It's the recipe that started it all—Nick's famous chile, lifted from a San Antonio, Texas, hotel restaurant. Outside of tweaking the spices mix to fit the Midwestern palate, the recipe and process for making Texas Tavern chile have remained the same these ninety years.

The secret to Texas Tavern's chile is in the brick of chili concentrate. These bricks contain the spice blend giving Tavern chile its unique flavor. Only the Bullingtons mix the spice recipe. The recipe itself is kept in a "secret location under lock and key," as I'm told. Both the spice mix and chili concentrate are made in bulk. The spice mix is kept in a container labeled "DO NOT TOUCH." The concentrate is divided into single, rectangular loaf pans with sliding lids for coverings (described once by *Roanoke Times* journalist Duncan Adams as a "primo casket for a hamster").

Note: The reader will notice two separate spellings of the word chili throughout the book. When referencing Texas Tavern's chile, it is spelled with an "e." When using the term "chili" in general, or as part of the Tavern's hot dog chili, it is spelled with an "i."

Texas Tavern chili concentrate in loaf pans. (Molly Bullington)

The chili concentrate and spice mix aren't the only ingredients that must be prepared in advance. The pinto beans, which come in fifty-pound sacks, must be thoroughly cleaned and soaked—usually overnight—in a twenty-quart stockpot. Once the beans are properly soaked they cook for around three and a half hours on a single gas-burner stove in the back of the Tavern. After this, the cooked beans must be drained and cooled. This is an exacting process. If not done properly, the entire batch is ruined. Indeed, preparing beans is so important employees must initial a small slip of paper and place it on top of each finished batch, claiming it as their own.

Finally, the starch must be premeasured. Employees scoop starch into tiny paper bags that look like they were made specifically for storing Tavern chile starch, or a few dozen jelly beans. Current owner Matt Bullington says he can always tell which employee measured and bagged any starch bag by the way it is folded, twisted, or otherwise closed.

With all these preparations in place, making an actual batch, as it's called in Tavern lingo, is no secret at all. But it is intense. Each step must happen in a particular order and precise manner. Without giving away secrets, here's how Texas Tavern chile is made:

1. Turn the gas burner to high.
2. Pull a brick of chili concentrate from the cooler. Use a metal stir spoon to scoop the concentrate from the loaf pan, taking care to scrape sides and corners, getting the container as clean as possible.
3. Add a premeasured amount of water to the chili concentrate.
4. Let water heat to a rolling boil. Stir occasionally as concentrate breaks up, melts, and combines with water.

Grill Man, Mike Witt, making a batch of chile during the Tavern's 80th Anniversary celebration, 2010.

5. While chili concentrate and water mixture is heating, fill a second metal measuring container with one heaping scoop of pinto beans.

6. Once chile comes to a rolling boil, prepare starch and water mix, whisking vigorously to ensure no clumping.

7. Add starch water to chile. Stir chile in a figure-eight pattern for forty-five seconds, with purpose—just shy of vigorous. *Note: The figure-eight pattern is important!*

8. Add the premeasured beans. Use the stir spoon to break the beans' fall into the chile, reducing splashing over sides of the pot.

9. Stir chile for another forty-five to sixty seconds until everything is well mixed.

10. Take the fresh-made batch out front yelling, *"Hot comin' through!"*

Passing on the Tavern Tradition

In 1938, my father, Harry Craighead, left the family farm at thirteen and came to the city to make money for the family. He modified his birth certificate to make him appear old enough for a job at the furniture factory and picked up any other work he could as well.

After WWII, many trains carrying soldiers home stopped briefly in Roanoke. Ever an enterprising young man, Dad would go to Texas Tavern and buy bags of hamburgers and sell them to the soldiers heading home. He made a small profit. But he always talked more about how great it was to see the soldiers enjoying their first restaurant hamburger they'd had in months.

I grew up going to Texas Tavern. I helped with the family business and my dad took me [to the T.T.] almost every Saturday and two or three times a week throughout summer. I live in North Carolina now, we make several trips to Roanoke each year just to go there. It was one of the first places I took my boyfriend—now my husband—for a date, even though we both lived in North Carolina at the time. It was even my daughter's requested meal this year for her fifteenth birthday.

Though my father died long before she was born, it's heartwarming to carry on this tradition with his granddaughter. I can picture him sitting next to her, ordering a bowl with and a cheesy western with.

—Laura Craighead, North Carolina

Dad and the "T-Room"

Forever Remembered: the "T-room:" My father worked hard, but money was always tight. Going to eat at Texas Tavern was a treat. I remember sitting on the stool when my feet didn't touch the foot rail. Before we paid, I'd add up our bill. My dad would ask me how much it was and then smile proudly at me when I got it right.

The reason I love Texas Tavern is because of my dad. He always loved a bowl with and burger all the way with a glass of buttermilk. Even as Alzheimer's stole his memory, anytime we went downtown he'd say, "That chili place" and delight in stopping by to eat.

A week before he died, I took Dad to a doctor's appointment downtown. He was so lost in the fog of his disease he didn't know his family anymore. When I tried to coax him off the exam table, he fearfully clung to it. I finally offered to take him to Texas Tavern for a bowl of chili if he would get down. His eyes lit up and he said, "Chili!" just like a kid hearing the ice cream truck.

He eagerly followed me to the car and got in. We went to the "T-room" and Dad gobbled up two bowls of chili and a hamburger. Then he didn't want to get off the stool! One of my last memories of my dad is him sitting on that stool, grinning ear to ear. It's a memory I will always cherish.

—Vicki Larrington, Roanoke

The hot with. (Molly Bullington)

THE HOT WITH

"Nobody, I mean, nobody puts ketchup on a hot dog."
Clint Eastwood
as Dirty Harry in *Sudden Impact*

"I keep my mouth wide open all the time,
A hot dog 'with' just tastes so mighty fine,
At Texas Tavern I save a dime."
Dan Casey
from his eighty-sixth Tavern birthday column,
spoofing on a famous Johnny Cash song

✪ ✪ ✪ ✪ ✪ ✪ ✪ ✪ ✪ ✪ ✪ ✪ ✪ ✪ ✪

Being an ignorant farm girl from Illinois, I always wondered what made a Coney Island hot dog different—and somehow special in my mind—from the Ball Park Franks my mother would occasionally buy at the grocery store. Even as an adult living for more than a decade "out East," as Midwesterners say, I still thought a Coney Island hot dog was something one could find only on Coney Island.

When I asked Matt Bullington what was so unique about Coney Island hot dogs—why this was the name Nick chose—he shrugged and said he wasn't sure. Maybe it's what everyone called hot dogs back when Nick opened the Tavern. Coney Island is where the hot dog was made famous. I nodded. We left it at that.

Except, I couldn't. I needed to understand why Nick Bullington, in his advertising genius, decided to call his hot dogs "Coney Island" hot dogs. Was it the type of wiener used? Was it the way in which the hot dog was made? Or was "Coney Island" another catchy phrase Nick harnessed, adding to the Tavern's quirkiness—like its other sayings about bumblebees and checks, or selling enough buttermilk to drown small horses?

After a much-too-involved Internet search, I determined the follow-ing: the Coney Island hot dog is a style. From Michigan . . . sort of. But it's named after Coney Island in New York, though the two styles—the Coney Island style and the style famous on Coney Island—are not the same.

Strange, I know.

In *The Great American Hot Dog Book*, author Becky Mercuri offers a survey of hot dog styles and top hot dog spots broken down by regions within the United States, the Texas Tavern being featured under the Southeast. She also gives a solid history of the American hot dog as we know it today.

Mercuri credits the enormous immigrant population of the late nine-teenth and early twentieth centuries, who saw the success of the Coney Island hot dog business and capitalized on the opportunity for them-selves. As immigrant groups moved to the various regions of the country, they created unique sauces to differentiate their hot dog businesses from one another. Mercuri makes special note of Greek immigrants, who were particularly savvy with building networks. They adapted their Old World recipes into new chili sauce recipes and renamed them "Coney Island" sauces. They would then share their recipes with family and friends opening restaurants in other locations. They named their hot dog shops "Coney Island" restaurants after the famous New York amusement park where they were first inspired to make the hot dog their own.

Mercuri places the Coney Island hot dog style squarely in the Mid-west—as well as at ballparks across America—giving special props to the Greek populations in Michigan. But even within the Midwest—par-ticularly in Michigan—Coney Island hot dog styles vary. Discussions surrounding such differences can become contentious, proving that not only barbeque in the South is capable of raising Cain.

What is the Coney Island hot dog style? It's a grilled hot dog served inside a warm, steamed bun and topped with chili sauce, chopped onions, and plain yellow mustard. This sounds a lot like a Texas Tavern hot with. Not surprising, given Nick Bullington's *and* the Texas Tavern's

Longtime Tavern employee, Danny Fralin, making a "hot with." (Shari Dragovich)

Midwestern roots. But like Coney Island hot dogs across the Midwest, the Texas Tavern hot with has its own particular style, too. To begin with, Tavern wieners are steamed, not grilled. Then, there is the Texas Tavern's proprietary chili sauce, a slightly altered version of the chili concentrate used to make Tavern chile. And, just as Greek families shared only amongst one another, the Bullingtons have carefully guarded the recipe to their hot dog chili sauce.

But the most distinctive feature to a Texas Tavern hot with is the addition of Tavern relish. You'd be hard pressed to find a version of Tavern relish anywhere in the Midwest. Maybe anywhere. More about Tavern relish in a later section. For now, understand this: Tavern relish is cabbage-based. There are no pickles in it. Cabbage, turned to colcslaw, screams Southern when it comes to toppings. It's what makes a hot with a true Texas Tavern original.

Imbibing Councilmen and Cross-eyed Countermen

I have been going to the T.T. since hamburgers, hot dogs, and chile were 10 cents apiece. We would skip school in the 1950s at Woodrow Wilson Jr. High and ride the bus to town to spend our lunch money at the Tavern.

There once was a city councilman who would come to the T.T. very late at night and sit at the last stool leaning against the wall and read the newspaper. He was known for imbibing quite a bit. He would occasionally rock back and forth before falling on the floor and everyone would help him back up on the stool, prop him against the wall, hand him his paper, and the night would continue.

Also, there once was a counter man who was seriously cross-eyed. He gave great service except when all the stools were packed you could not tell who he was looking at asking for their order or asking what you had when you wanted to pay.

—Stuart Boblett, Roanoke

JOYS AND CHALLENGES OF A 1930s KITCHEN

"The Tavern kitchen? It's the height of low tech."
Matt Bullington
fourth-generation Texas Tavern owner

✪ ✪ ✪ ✪ ✪ ✪ ✪ ✪ ✪ ✪ ✪ ✪ ✪ ✪ ✪

I opened the door to the back half of the Texas Tavern and was met with a giant sack of onions at my feet. In front of me was an organization system of built-in, white painted cabinets and cubby spaces reminiscent of an old-time mercantile wall. There was nowhere for me to turn but right. So, I did.

Welcome to the back of the Texas Tavern, where chile dreams are made. It's a space organized into three medium-sized walk-in closets placed one behind the other, a small doorway—without the door—connecting each section. Two parts of the space are original; the last walk-in closet space is an addition built during the second Bullington generation of Tavern existence. It's office, pantry, equipment storage, and kitchen all in one. The space directly behind the back wall of the Tavern's dining area is where most of the cooking and food prep happen. When I stand facing the stove and put my arms out, I can easily touch both walls. There is a tiny closet bathroom at one end of the space. The original three-burner kitchen range is set at the other end. The piping is exposed and painted the same color as the walls. Every square-inch of nook and cranny space is utilized. Even the worn-smooth concrete floor.

Like the rest of the Tavern, much of the tools and equipment find their origins in the 1930s, too: the cast-iron Griswold stovetop—which Matt works on himself—pots, measuring cups, all the cubbies, all the cabinets. It's a quintessential 1930s utilitarian kitchen space.

The Griswold stove in the Texas Tavern kitchen. (Shari Dragovich)

Working in the Texas Tavern kitchen can be its own kind of workout. There are giant sacks of pinto beans, onions, and cabbage that must be unloaded, maneuvered through the tiny back space, and stacked out of the way. Supplies and ingredients are also stored high overhead, requiring an Olympic-style lift to put things away. Food prep happens on a single three-foot-long metal work counter. Everything from dicing onions, chopping cabbage, and allowing that twenty-quart pot of cooked pinto beans to finish draining happens in a space not much larger than a cutting board.

To watch employees move and work throughout the back spaces of the Tavern is really something. Two bodies are about all the area can handle well. And, since the Tavern never closes, all the deliveries, food prep, cleaning—in short, *everything*—must be done while still serving customers. And they do it! Most of the time it looks like the smooth efficiency of an assembly line. Sometimes it looks more like a swarm of bumblebees. Always it works.

Yet another marvel of the Texas Tavern.

Behind the Counter

I started bagging crackers at age two. I made fifteen cents a box. I worked at the Tavern from age ten to twenty-eight with my dad. In the 1970s I worked the night shift. A lot of the guys were alcoholics, but don't get me wrong, these guys could retain orders and give correct change. If you couldn't add, subtract, and take orders, you weren't going to work there.

Carlton West—long-time Tavern employee—had a scar on his face. When someone would come in and start giving him a hard time late at night, Carlton would look at the guy and point to his scar and say, "Do you think I got this scar from playing marbles?" That would always diffuse the situation.

Henry Cox one time threw his shoe at some guy at the Tavern who was trying to cause trouble one night. The guy broke off a fan blade and was going after Henry with it. Henry ran around the counter with only one shoe on and a Coke bottle. He was going after that guy!

One time, in the late 70s when my dad was on vacation and I was working the day shift, I got a call in the middle of the night from a customer who was at the Tavern and saw there were no workers. I had to get up and get dressed and go down there. A couple customers stayed to keep watch over things until I could get there. I worked four days straight, twenty-four hours a day for ninety-six hours. After my dad got home, he asked me how everything went, and I said, "Fine," because it was actually kinda normal, you know? Down at the Tavern, what is normal? You gotta ask yourself, what is normal?"

—*Steve Barbour, Buchanan, Virginia*

Texas Tavern

2ND GEN

J.G. BULLINGTON

Good work is always modestly scaled, for it cannot ignore either the nature of individual places or the differences between places.

WENDELL BERRY

This generation of Americans has a rendezvous with destiny.

FRANKLIN DELANO ROOSEVELT
in his speech accepting renomination
June 27, 1936

James Gladstone Bullington, second generation Texas Tavern owner, ca. 1927.

While Nick was in Virginia making a second go of his Texas Tavern, Cassie and James—called Jim and then J. G. as an adult—were still living in Huntington, West Virginia. Details are obscure, but sometime late in their son's childhood, Nick and Cassie had a falling out and eventually divorced.

Nick and Cassie's breakup altered the course of J. G.'s life. J. G. longed to enroll full time at Culver Military Academy, a private military-style boarding school located in northern Indiana. He'd spent at least one summer of his youth at Culver Academy Camp—a time he recollected with great fondness through the rest of his life. But with his parents' separation, J. G.'s dream was never realized. Instead of military academy, J. G. finished high school in Huntington and went to work for, and then managed, an auto-parts store.

"He always regretted not going to college," recollected David Bullington, cousin to current owner Matt Bullington.

David, Matt, and I were sitting outside under the covered area of a local coffee shop in South County, Roanoke. I was meeting with David specifically for mining details of J. G.'s life. David occupies a unique position of knowing when it comes to some Bullington family history. As a lawyer, David helped his Uncle Jim—Matt's father, third-generation Tavern owner—go through boxes of old family files after J. G. passed away. He's also more than ten years Matt's senior, so his recollections of J. G. are clearer than Matt's own. We met on one of those paradoxically warm fall days; leaves were falling from trees, but folks were wearing summer attire. The conversation and weather conditions—easy, open, and meandering—made for a perfect traipse down memory lane.

"He was a phenomenal writer," said David of his grandfather, the second generation Bullington to own the Texas Tavern. "He had a superb vocabulary. He was a very intelligent guy who never made it past high school."

Not only was J. G. witty and smart, he was also a true child of the age into which he was born—the automobile era. J. G. was a true car aficionado. Since, according to Matt, Huntington always identified more as an Ohio River Valley town, and because of family ties to Indiana, J. G.

grew up an Indy race-car man at heart. As soon as he could manage to set his feet on the ground, J. G. rode motorcycles. He owned more than one Indian motorcycle. He was known for driving the coolest cars and driving them on the most serpentine roads he could find. J. G. was also known for being persnickety about his cool cars.

"Pawpaw was very particular about his cars," said Matt. "I always remembered the story about him, that he would take his car to the shop, pay for an oil change, but then insist on doing it himself. Right there in the shop. He was so meticulous about his car, he wouldn't let anyone else change the oil."

J. G. didn't love all automobiles. He loved a particular type of automobile. While Ford and Chevrolet were duking it out for the American public's affections, J. G. would have none of it. His heartstrings tugged for the M.G.—a British-made automobile best known for its two-seat, open sports cars. David remembers J. G. owning several different models of the M.G: the "A," the Magnette, and even the "T." Not only was this unique amongst his peers, it was an odd love, practically speaking. J. G. was not a small man.

J. G. loved driving his cool cars around town and across Appalachia to the old farmstead in Paris, Illinois, which J. G. inherited after Nick's passing. And, like most boys of the automobile era, he loved tinkering with his cars, too.

In fact, tinkering was one of J. G.'s favorite pastimes. Whether with one of his cars, or some project he'd putter with during his summers spent on the Illinois farm, or the old houseboat he kept out at Smith Mountain Lake, for J. G. it was more about the process rather than the end result.

While Nick was moving his Tavern from the Midwest to the Southeast, nineteen-year-old J. G. was fully immersed in his own life, managing the auto-parts store and dating Elizabeth "Libby" Merritt, a petite young woman with a giant personality whose family had deep roots throughout the Ohio River Valley. In 1931—a year into the Roanoke Tavern's existence—J. G. and Libby were married in Huntington. They were both twenty years old and "quite the pair," as expressed by multiple Bullington family members. J. G. also became an instant father to Libby's toddling son, Fred, her one blessing from a short first marriage to one of J. G.'s Huntington buddies. A

year after they were married, J. G. accepted a job in St. Petersburg, Florida, running another auto-parts store. While the young Bullington family was adjusting to life at sea level, the two-year-old Texas Tavern was finding its new mountain digs quite agreeable. By 1934, Nick was ready to expand.

For years, J. G.'s relationship with his father had been strained. Nick's restless entrepreneurial wanderings and eventual split with Cassie made him not an absent father-figure per se, but somewhat of an uneven one. And yet, as David recounted to me, J. G. adored his dad.

"J. G. clearly idolized his father," David said. "Going through all his old stuff, I really came to understand this. I mean, he saved every single scrap of paper from his father. My perspective is that he loved his dad. He idolized him, even if he felt like he lived in his dad's shadow somewhat."

Not only did J. G. keep every scrap of paper and memento of his father's, he added to the pile. By the time J. G. passed away, he left boxes and boxes

J. G. and Libby Bullington, ca. 1933.

of memories for his children and grandchildren to sift through and sort. This was a man loyal to his family down to his bones.

Maybe this was why J. G. didn't hesitate when Nick wrote him from Roanoke with an offer to run a second Texas Tavern location he'd opened in Lynchburg, Virginia. Nick had been managing both restaurants himself, driving back and forth between Roanoke and Lynchburg—a drive not nearly as easy in the 1930s as it is today. J. G. accepted his father's offer. By the end of 1934, J. G., Libby, and Fred had traded their seaside life for the rolling hills of Lynchburg.

J. G. ran the Lynchburg Tavern identically to the Roanoke location. The two diners were nearly the same, with the Lynchburg Tavern enjoying a slightly roomier inside. But, in keeping with Nick's fascination with the future of standardization, the two Taverns were mirror images of one another, even down to Nick's lucky number for his Lynchburg Tavern's opening day: the thirteenth day of the month.

The Bullingtons carried on this way for several years: Nick at the Roanoke Tavern, J. G. owning and operating the Lynchburg Tavern. By 1938, however, Nick's health was failing him. He'd lived a full life to be sure, but one that hadn't lent itself to longevity into old age. With his father no longer able to work, J. G. began managing both Taverns. This didn't last long. Jim soon wearied of the constant driving. He had two small children at home: Fred and a new baby, James Newton. The economy still staggered under the weight of the Depression. Another war loomed, and with it the inevitable rationing that would undoubtedly hit the food industry. For all these reasons, J. G. decided to sell the Lynchburg Tavern. He would move his family to Roanoke and focus his energies on the Roanoke Texas Tavern instead. However, he wasn't willing to leave the Lynchburg Tavern to just anyone. Trusting his father's business affinities towards the Tavern's first manager still living in the Midwest, J. G. sent word to Charles Van Cleve, offering him first dibs at ownership. Van Cleve accepted J. G.'s offer. In 1940, the Van Cleve family moved to Lynchburg, where they owned and operated the Lynchburg Tavern from 1940 until it eventually closed in 1969 after Van Cleve's death. Katherine Van Cleve—Charles Van Cleve's wife—sold the equipment and business to a new owner, who converted an old gas station up the street and reopened the restaurant as the Texas Inn. The original Tavern building was razed a decade or so after the Van Cleves sold it as part of the government's decades-long urban renewal project.

While there are many similarities in menu and style between the Roanoke Texas Tavern and Lynchburg's Texas Inn, they are not the same. The recipes have been altered over the years and the restaurant itself has changed ownership several times. The most noticeable difference is that the Texas Inn sells french fries. Similar to the Texas Tavern, however, is the Texas Inn's beloved status among Lynchburg residents and its important role in adding to its town's culture.

✪ ✪ ✪ ✪ ✪ ✪ ✪ ✪ ✪ ✪ ✪ ✪ ✪ ✪ ✪

On the afternoon of December 2, 1943, at the age of sixty-six, Nick Bullington passed away. According to his obituary, Nick died "suddenly" in his home at 345 West Church Avenue, a property he owned a few blocks from the Tavern—a property that would eventually become a critical piece of the Tavern's story. Nick was survived by his new wife, Mary, a mystery woman the Bullingtons know little of; his son, James Gladstone; and three grandchildren, one of whom—James Newton—was destined to become the Tavern's third generational owner.

Though exact timing is unknown, J. G. moved his mother, Cassie, to Roanoke, adding to the Bullington presence in southwest Virginia. She moved into the house on Church Avenue, which J. G. inherited after Nick's death. Cassie lived the rest of her days in Roanoke, watching her son and his family—as well as the Texas Tavern—grow and prosper. Though the exact date of her passing is unknown, Katherine Wise Bullington lived well into her eighties, passing away in the early 1960s.

✪ ✪ ✪ ✪ ✪ ✪ ✪ ✪ ✪ ✪ ✪ ✪ ✪ ✪ ✪

From the time Nick Bullington opened the Texas Tavern to the year of his death, the United States moved from the catastrophes of a countrywide depression to being entrenched in a second world war. As with the Depression, Roanoke fared far better than much of the country during World War II, thanks once again to Norfolk and Western Railroad. According to local historian Nelson Harris, between Roanoke's railroad industry and its airport, the city continued its trajectory of upward mobility, even through wartime America. I met with Harris to gain a better picture of Roanoke's—and thus the Texas Tavern's—economy and community life during the decades of the 1940s through the 1950s. At the time of our meeting, Harris was himself in the middle of research for his latest book project, *The Roanoke Valley in the 1940s*, a weekly review of Roanoke history from that era.

"Rationing ground everything to a halt," Harris explained to me on a rainy afternoon as we sat protected on his sunporch, but still a part of the light autumn rain.

"Except in Roanoke," he then qualified. "In Roanoke, we had Mr. Woodrum."

Clifton A. Woodrum was a local pharmacist, lawyer, and US representative who staunchly supported the efforts of President Roosevelt during the Depression and World War II. He was also a fierce promoter of all things benefitting Virginia, and especially his hometown, Roanoke. In 1930, Woodrum petitioned hard for government funding to make needed improvements to Roanoke's airport, which, at that time, included a couple of dirt runways and a small room atop a nearby farmhouse that acted as the control tower.

But Woodrum didn't stop there. He petitioned for Roanoke's airport to become one of the government's National Defense Projects. This allowed the airport to receive federal funding, eventually making Roanoke a key player in the war.

"Once the Pacific broke out, aircraft were being built on the East Coast," said Harris. "They would come off the assembly line, fly to Roanoke for fueling up, then fly on."

Harris had several proofs of Roanoke's position of importance during the war. For instance, during World War II, Roanoke had more air traffic than Dulles and La Guardia combined. There was also the day in 1943 when Roanoke's airport was the second busiest on the planet. The military decided to locate a naval aviation cadet-training center in Roanoke. Finally, because of the combined powers of railroad and airport, Roanoke became a major ferrying station for both troops and supplies through the entirety of the war.

In the midst of all this, there was the Texas Tavern, playing its part in feeding those men, women, and families caught up in the movement and saga of war. Even through the trials of rationed supplies, J. G. and Libby held the Tavern in steady business.

J. G. managed the Tavern's day-to-day operations. He had a special fondness for his employees and is remembered by his family as being incredibly committed to their well-being. Indeed, it was partly J. G.'s compassion for his employees that rubbed off on his son Jim, influencing Jim's lifelong practice of always offering both his customers and his employees "a fair shake."

Libby, known as "Miz B." by Tavern employees, kept the aprons and hats starched and mended. She also contributed plenty of big personality to the Tavern atmosphere. She was called a "spitfire" by all who knew her. She, too, liked her fast, small sports cars. Matt remembers the Mazda 929 she bought herself, which Matt was allowed to drive only once. Velma Bullington, Matt's mother and Libby's daughter-in-law, described Libby as "four-foot-ten and full of sass."

"Gram stayed forever young in her own mind," said Velma. "She also had almost no filter. As she got older, she lost her filter altogether. . . . We disagreed on almost every point and couldn't have been more opposite in our personalities. And she was the best mother-in-law I could have ever asked for."

Together, J. G. and Libby, with their large personalities and cool little sports cars, kept right on going through the challenges of wartime America. They raised their three children and continued to be quite the pair, even as they kept the Texas Tavern going strong.

✪ ✪ ✪ ✪ ✪ ✪ ✪ ✪ ✪ ✪ ✪ ✪ ✪ ✪ ✪

One of J. G.'s favorite maxims in life was "If it ain't broke, don't fix it." This was a tenet he applied to all things, but especially to his management of the Texas Tavern. In some ways, it was this most simple maxim that propelled the Tavern from ordinary burger joint to eventual cultural mooring. J. G. believed emphatically in his father's business model. He continued Nick's pithy marketing strategies with his own quirky spin. He kept a simple but meticulous paperwork system. J. G. believed in the simplicity of simple things. If Nick was the typecast of the twentieth-century entrepreneur, J. G. was the typecast of its preserver.

In the decades after the war, Roanoke's boomtown status spiked. Throughout the 1940s and into the 1950s, Roanoke boasted a population twice that of Charlotte, North Carolina. All the area's businesses located their office centers downtown. Norfolk and Western, Appalachian Power, Roanoke City's school administrative offices, all the banks—these were but a few of the names attached to the sides of Roanoke's downtown buildings. Along with this was a vibrant downtown shopping district with several department stores, independent retailers, doctor's offices, and more.

J. G. on his Indian, ca. 1928.

As a result, the Texas Tavern enjoyed several vibrant economic decades with J. G. at the helm, maintaining its integrity and service to Roanokers with very few changes. J. G. and Libby embedded themselves in the Roanoke community. J. G. continued the Bullington tradition of serving as a Mason in a local Roanoke chapter. With his commitment to his customers, his employees, and his staunch belief in not fiddling with things not broken, J. G. Bullington took the Texas Tavern from quick-bite diner to Roanoke mainstay. He stewarded the Tavern until his health began to deteriorate in the late 1960s. After passing the chili spice recipe, as well as all the other Tavern's food secrets, onto his son, Jim, J. G. retired his Tavern apron. He passed away on September 21, 1985, at the age of seventy-four. Libby lived well past her husband, forever young until her death in 2004.

Training Up the Next Generation

I have been a customer at Texas Tavern for years. As my children grew, I would get food to go and we would eat at home. One night, my teenaged daughter went with me to pick up the food. As we walked in, one of the other customers graciously slid over to give us two seats together and invited us to sit down. My daughter announced we were only there to get takeout. A customer began schooling her on enjoying the "full experience" at Texas Tavern, while my daughter stood there turning red with embarrassment. Now when we mention Texas Tavern I ask, "Takeout or full experience?"

—Barney Woody, Roanoke

THE CHEESY WESTERN

"I can't get no, Cheesy Western,
I can't get no, Cheesy Western,
Well I tried, and I tried,
And I tried, and I tried,
I can't get no dum, dum, dum,
I can't get no dum, dum, dum . . ."

Dan Casey

in an eighty-sixth Tavern birthday tribute, spoofing a song he said
Mick Jagger composed after coming to the T.T. and finding it out of eggs.

"Ahhhh! There is nothing like a cheesy western and a bowl of Texas Tavern
chili to get the wheels turning. . . . Having just ingested my monthly
ration of brain food, I am in the mood to write a masterpiece."

Mike Ives

from his *Roanoke Times* column (1973)

✪ ✪ ✪ ✪ ✪ ✪ ✪ ✪ ✪ ✪ ✪ ✪ ✪ ✪ ✪

Though J. G. hated change, there was one major change he
made early in his stewardship of the Texas Tavern: the addition of the
cheesy western. The cheesy western is an iteration of the Texas Tavern's
western sandwich, a menu item on the Tavern's wall from its beginning.
J. G. simply added cheese to the egg-and-hamburger sandwich.

It would take decades before the cheesy western captured the hearts
and minds of Roanokers. After the Great Depression and then wartime
rationing, Americans were shy of the excesses of life. But somewhere
in the mid- to late 1970s, the cheesy western slowly grew in status.
Just like fashion, music, and free time, it seems taste buds trend, too.
The "cheesy," as it's called in official Tavern language, is now one of the
Tavern's most popular menu items and has garnered much national
attention. It has been featured in: *Garden and Gun, Country Living, Taste*

The Cheesy Western. (Don Petersen)

of the South, *Money Magazine, Car and Driver, Lonely Planet, Fodor's, Let's Go*, major newspapers for the cities of Charlotte, Richmond, and Atlanta, and multiple travel guides. It also made the cut in John T. Edge's *Southern Belly* and all three editions of George Motz's *Hamburger America*.

Matt thinks *Roanoke Times* journalist Mike Ives—however unintentionally—had some influence on the increasing popularity of the cheesy western. Ives loved the Texas Tavern and often wrote about it in his column. He especially loved the cheesy western. Naturally, the cheesy western made it into Ives's columns with some regularity, either overtly or by sliding it in the backdoor while telling one of his Tavern tales. Whether it was Ives's influence or the culture's evolving taste buds or a little of both, by the mid-1980s, the Tavern sold more cheesys than it had in all the Tavern's decades combined.

Grill Man, Cecil Spradin, making a Cheesy Western. (Molly Bullington)

Tavern employees like to say making a cheesy isn't "rocket science." Maybe it's not rocket science, but it does take a certain culinary mastery at the grill. There is a particular order and way for making a cheesy western. Not following this way is to cause all kinds of trouble—from backed-up orders to egg on only half the sandwich or a less-than-gooey melted-cheese goodness in every bite.

There is also no end to the variations on the cheesy western, and everyone has his or her favorite way. Most common is the "cheesy with," followed closely by the "double meat cheesy," and then the plain "cheesy." Matt likes his cheesy western double meat with hot dog chili and Tavern relish. In his book *Hamburger America*, George Motz writes

TEXAS TAVERN: FOUR GENERATIONS OF THE MILLIONAIRES CLUB

that his cheesy "sweet spot" includes three patties, the scrambled egg, and all the regular toppings: cheese, pickle, onion, relish, and mustard along with a dollop of Texas Tavern hot dog chili. My own cheesy preference is similar to Matt's, minus one hamburger patty and the addition of chopped onions.

It's hard to imagine the cheesy western falling from its fabled state of popularity. And yet, just as the Texas Tavern's old-timers prove, tastes do collectively change. It makes one wonder what might someday replace the cheesy western in popularity. Whatever it is, the future star of the Texas Tavern menu already exists, embedded in the menu. It's only waiting to be discovered, or maybe returned to.

The Tavern's Reach

I live in Baltimore and my ex-wife is from Roanoke. Starting in the late 1970s, we made frequent trips to Roanoke to visit my in-laws. Many folks don't realize the national and perhaps global reach the phenomenon of Texas Tavern has.

I spent my career in the high-tech business and worked in the early 2000s for a company called PeopleSoft, headquartered in Silicon Valley. We had an annual conference in San Francisco. One year I was talking to a colleague from headquarters and somehow he mentioned that he grew up in Roanoke. I told him my connection to Roanoke. He smiled and asked, "Do you like your bowl with or without?" We both had a good laugh.

Texas Tavern means a lot to me. Places like it are endangered species. They are getting more and more rare. Besides, I like the chili!

—*Chuck Piel, Ellicott City, Maryland*

ON SISSY SAUCE
AND TAVERN RELISH

"Everyone knows you don't put ketchup on a good hamburger."
Matt Bullington
fourth-generation Texas Tavern owner

✪ ✪ ✪ ✪ ✪ ✪ ✪ ✪ ✪ ✪ ✪ ✪ ✪ ✪ ✪

On Sissy Sauce: One of the first quirks I learned about the Texas Tavern is they don't serve ketchup. At least, not without some harassment from employees behind the counter.

When the Tavern opened in 1930, ketchup wasn't a common condiment for hamburgers or hot dogs. The famous Coney Island hot dog was slathered in chili, onions, and mustard. White Castle sold their sliders most commonly with onions and pickle. And while Henry J. Heinz's commercial version of ketchup had long since released the homemaker from making and canning it herself—the Heinz Ketchup Company being established in 1876—still, ketchup remained more of a novelty item than household staple.

It wasn't until fast food restaurants began making french fries and serving ketchup as a dipping sauce that ketchup exploded. Naturally, this led to people putting ketchup on their hamburgers, then their hot dogs, and then everything else.

From its inception, the Texas Tavern has been a mustard-only establishment. Not regular mustard, mind you. Tavern mustard is special. In yet another proprietary secret, Texas Tavern mustard is doctored with a little something giving it an extra zip of tastiness. As the rest of America started giving way to the ketchup craze, the Texas Tavern held strong. For decades, the Bullingtons stood by their "no ketchup" policy, insisting ketchup masks the flavor of food and only mustard—especially

Texas Tavern mustard—brings it out. This worked well until fast food finally made its way through an entire generation. Kids started coming in asking for ketchup, intolerant of a burger joint in America that didn't serve it. Finally, Gordon Barbour, general manager under Jim's third generation of Tavern ownership, began bringing ketchup packets into work. He'd only give the packets out when a child asked, and even then he'd try to give it on the sly. If adults asked for ketchup, he'd give some vague answer about the Tavern not serving ketchup.

Of course, this caused conflict. You can't very well tell one customer there's no ketchup while you're handing ketchup packets to another—under twelve years old or not. But adding ketchup to the counter was unthinkable. It's the sort of thing that would have fundamentally altered the identity and personality of the Texas Tavern. This was one of those difficult Tavern moments: how to adjust to the changing times and yet remain the same. It's a complicated dance, and one the Bullingtons have had to contend with many times through the decades.

The quiet ketchup distribution—and subsequent growing dispute—went on for several years, right into Matt Bullington's era of Tavern ownership. Matt knew something must be done. Ketchup was here to stay. The Tavern needed a tactful way of dealing with it. He had an idea: what if they kept the ketchup packets on hand but hidden? If the customer asking for ketchup looked older than twelve years old, the counterman was obligated to rib the person a bit—good naturedly, of course—calling the ketchup "sissy sauce" and saying they don't typically serve the stuff to anyone over twelve. Matt took his new policy idea to his father, Jim, who was in partial retirement at that point. He asked for his father's thoughts and, hopefully, his blessing. Jim consented, so long as there was never ketchup kept on the counter. He found it a wise middle ground for an otherwise untenable situation. The ketchup ribbing has worked so well it's now one of Roanokers' favorite practical jokes to play on unsuspecting friends and visitors. Send them to the Tavern and tell them to ask for a bunch of ketchup to go with their burger. Oh, and ask for fries, too.

Tavern Relish, pickles, and onions. (Molly Bullington)

Tavern Relish: What the Tavern doesn't offer in the typical fast food restaurant it more than makes up for in Tavern relish. It is one more way it sets itself apart.

Texas Tavern relish is proprietary. You won't find it anywhere else on the planet. You'll find a close likeness to it an hour east at the Lynchburg Texas Inn. But it's not the same. And, yes, like the chile, it has its secret ingredients. But what is most impressive about Tavern relish, besides taste, is the effort involved in making it. The relish that tops every "cheesy with" and "hot all the way" takes hours to make and is labor intensive.

As mentioned earlier, Tavern relish is cabbage-based. Each batch of Tavern relish—made two to three times a week—uses an entire fifty-pound bag of cabbages. These must be cleaned and sliced down several times to a size amenable for running through the meat grinder used only for grinding cabbage. The grinder itself is persnickety. It's bulky for the small space where it's used. It also requires some physical effort to push the cabbage through without clogging its mechanics.

The ground cabbage drops straight through from the grinder into the waiting mixture of wet ingredients set underneath it. Once all the cabbage has been run through the grinder, it must be mixed thoroughly with the wet ingredients. This process is all part of the proprietary Tavern relish secret.

Start to finish, the process of making Tavern relish takes from one to two hours. Like every other job at the Tavern, it must be done in between serving customers and maintaining other front-of-the-house jobs. I haven't met a Tavern employee yet whose favorite task is making Tavern relish. But I also haven't met any not proud of their role in keeping alive the Tavern relish tradition.

Tavern Initiations

My husband, Rick, moved to Roanoke from Hampton, Virginia, after college. After a night of drinking with his coworker, Randy, who was born and raised in Roanoke, they went to T.T. Not wanting to appear a newbie, my husband ordered a cheesy western and a bowl with, just as Randy had done. They ate the chili and when my husband bit into his burger, in a loud voice, exclaimed, "This SOB has an egg on it!" Everyone roared.

—Jayne Ashe, South Carolina

SIGNS, SAYINGS, AND THE SECRET MENU

"We Seat 1,000 PEOPLE—10 AT A TIME."

"We don't CASH CHECKS or play with BUMBLE BEES."

"Yes, ladies enjoy eating here."

✪ ✪ ✪ ✪ ✪ ✪ ✪ ✪ ✪ ✪ ✪ ✪ ✪ ✪ ✪

It's one of the first things that alert you to the different-ness of the place you just walked into: the signs and sayings covering both inside and outside the Texas Tavern's walls.

"OPEN ALL NITE" says the white lettering painted directly on the windows using all capital letters in simple font. All over the outside walls, there are signs declaring what one will find on the inside: "Coney Island Hot Dogs," "Mexican Chile," and "Cold Buttermilk." There's a sign on the glass door declaring, "Yes, ladies enjoy eating here," also in simple block lettering, with the "Yes" written in Tavern red.

Once inside, the quirky signs continue: "We Seat 1,000 PEOPLE—10 AT A TIME." "We don't CASH CHECKS or play with BUMBLE BEES." "Please Pay When Served." "$5.00 FREE if you are not offered a receipt showing the correct amount of your purchase." No matter where you turn there's a funny little saying or important notice for your eye to catch.

But it's what you hear when you step inside the Texas Tavern that is just as much a curiosity:

"Two hots with, and a bowl with!"

"One cheesy, one hot, and a bowl, walkin'!"

"Hot, just chili!"

"Hey, put on a batch!"

Yes, ladies enjoy eating here too. (Molly Bullington)

What is this crazy language? And why does it seem everyone—customers and employees alike—understands it?

It's Texas Tavern lingo.

From its beginning, the Texas Tavern has had its own quirky lingo for ordering. You won't see this language anywhere on the menu board. It's one of those things folks pick up over time and patient teaching from employees. The basic rundown looks like this:

A bowl: an eight-ounce bowl of chile. That would be the "Mexican Chile" advertised on the wall outside.

A bowl with: bowl of chile with chopped onions.

Cheesy with: cheesy western and all its toppings—Tavern relish, mustard, pickles—with onion.

Cheesy without: same as above, except no onions.

Cheesy plain: cheesy western without any toppings.

The famous "We Seat 1,000 people . . . 10 at a time" sign. (Molly Bullington)

Hot with: hot dog with all its toppings—Tavern relish, mustard, hot dog chili—and onions.

Hot without: same as above, except no onions.

Hot just chili: hot dog with only chili topping.

One: hamburger (or *two*, or *three* . . . any number by itself indicates hamburgers).

One with: hamburger with onions.

Add a slab: add cheese.

Walking: order is to-go.

If you recognize a pattern, it's because there is one. You start with whatever the menu item is and then add from there. "With" always means everything on it, plus onions. If you've ever been to Philadelphia for an authentic Philly cheesesteak, you'll recognize the similarities.

While the Tavern's menu lingo adds to the unique atmosphere of the place, it exists for practical reasons. Since employees don't write down orders at the Tavern, there must be a quick and consistent system for conveying orders to whoever is working the grill. Along with this, the grill person needs an easy way to track what he's making. This becomes critical during high volume times, weekend nights at 2:30 A.M., in particular.

If you hear someone order something that resembles none of the above—like a "Diesel Dog" or a "911"—you've just been given a glimpse into the Tavern's secret menu. Matt says the secret menu is an underground series of menu items that has evolved over the last five to ten years, mostly from regular customers' unique ordering habits. There's the Travis, named after a once-local bartender who would come into the Tavern after his night shift. It involves putting a slice of grilled ham on a cheesy western. A Dirty Travis is a Travis with hot dog chili added. There's the 911, also known as the Jumbo Jimbo, named after a gentleman who worked downtown and frequented the Tavern for lunch. It's also what one will likely need after eating it. A Jumbo Jimbo—or 911, whichever you prefer—is two double-meat cheesy westerns stacked on top of one another. And then there's the Diesel Dog, which is a cheesy

Another famous sign at Texas Tavern. (Molly Bullington)

western and a hot dog union: a hot dog wrapped in an egg with cheese and then nestled in the bun. No one remembers how the Diesel Dog got its name.

There's one other turn of phrase that is classic to the Texas Tavern, and it's arguably the most important. The Tavern is known as "The Millionaires Club." Simply put, it's a place that has no respect for the hierarchies of life. As Jim Bullington said to a *Roanoke Times* reporter back in 2005, "You don't have to be a millionaire to come in the Texas Tavern, but everybody is going to be treated like they are when they come through the door. I don't care if you're broke or whether you own one of the largest corporations in the city, everybody is treated the same."

Famous Tavern Visitors: Real and Perceived

One proof of the Texas Tavern's rare qualities is the number of famous visitors it has attracted through the decades. The list of actual sightings is impressive. When one adds Roanoke Times *columnist Dan Casey's cast of visitors from his anniversary columns, it's downright fantastical. Here's a list, broken down by "Verified" and "Hey, it's possible!"*

Verified:
Vice President Mike Pence (then governor)
Harry Connick Jr. has literally sung T.T.'s praises in concert
Kevin Costner, who was glad to be treated like a "regular guy" by T.T.'s employees
Michael Feldman, who practiced his Tavern ordering all night before going at 2 A.M.
The Glen Miller Band • Julius "Dr. J" Erving • Aaron Neville
Senator Mark Warner • The Three Stooges (visited the Lynchburg Tavern)
David Huddleston • Members of Crosby, Stills, Nash & Young
Former Virginia governors Lynwood Holton and Terry McAuliffe
Former congressmen Caldwell Butler and Bob Goodlatte

Hey, it's possible!:
President Donald Trump
Muhammad Ali (strong evidence for, but not fully verified)
Rod Stewart (also strong evidence for, but unverified)
Elvis Presley • Johnny Cash • Mick Jagger • James Brown

Texas Tavern

3RD GEN

JIM BULLINGTON

A good man out of the good treasure of the heart bringeth forth good things.

MATTHEW 12:35

You have not lived today until you have done something for someone who can never repay you.

JOHN BUNYAN

James Newton Bullington, third generation Texas Tavern owner, ca. 1964.

Thanks to J. G.'s personal motto to leave things well enough alone, the Texas Tavern remained essentially unchanged through the decades following World War II. This was unique during a time when change in America abounded. And yet J. G. was undeterred, even as Roanoke's downtown continued its transformation into a booming, modernized metropolis. Thus, by the time J. G.'s son Jim took over management of the Tavern, it was no longer simply a restaurant. It had become a microcosm of days gone by. James Newton Bullington, better known as "Jim," was born September 12, 1938. He was the middle of J. G. and Libby's three children, with Fred being the older and Kay being the younger. Jim's childhood consisted of all the usual boyhood things for a child growing up in postwar America. It also included a run-in with one of its life-threatening ailments: polio.

Around the age of eleven, Jim came down with polio while spending the summer with his mother's family in Huntington, West Virginia. He was placed in a ward with other severely sick children, many of them with terminal conditions. For a time, doctors didn't think Jim would survive. They were certain he would never walk again. J. G. and Libby moved their son home as soon as he could be safely transported. Jim did recover but remained physically weakened by the disease, a trial for any young boy, but especially for a boy being raised in the 1950s. Not only did polio leave Jim weak, it also created in him a compassion for those less fortunate. As soon as he was able, Jim made it a point to visit other children—many of them his friends—in the hospital, fighting to survive. He didn't shy away from the worst cases, not even those children being kept alive in iron lungs. Not even those he knew wouldn't survive. The illness and experience would change Jim forever. It seared in him a deep tender-heartedness for the less fortunates in life and a conviction to forever be their advocate.

It took years, but Jim did make a full recovery from polio. He attended Hargrave Military Academy in Chatham, Virginia, for his middle school years. It seems Jim was so mischievous while at Hargrave he earned himself hours upon hours of walking demerits, even earning the school's

Jim and Paul Starkey, ca. 1944.

Jim on his motorcycle while in Japan, ca. 1968.

demerit record—a title he held until somewhere in the mid-2000s. As an adult, Jim would joke that earning the Hargrave demerit record was the best thing to ever happen to him. All that walking strengthened his legs. Jim came back to Roanoke for high school good as new.

What polio didn't affect one iota was Jim's appetite for independence. Whetting this appetite even more was the cantankerous relationship he and J. G. shared. In 1956, at the age of seventeen—before graduating high school—Jim left home and joined the Air Force. He served four years: six months in San Antonio for training, then three and a half years in Japan, in Nagasaki and Okinawa. He did administrative work. For years afterwards Jim would joke that he went into the Air Force to fly airplanes and spent four years flying a typewriter instead. At any rate, while back in San Antonio after his time in Japan, Jim met his wife, Velma, at a Christmas party the night before he was set to move home to Roanoke.

As the story goes, it was December 1959. Jim was spending his last night in San Antonio at a holiday party at Fort Sam Houston. His bags were packed. He was set for moving home. But after the party, Jim went back to his room and began unpacking his bags, putting t-shirts and socks back in drawers.

"What are you doin'?" his roommate asked.

"I just met the woman I'm going to marry," Jim replied. That was that.

On June 1, 1960, Jim, at the age of twenty-one, and Velma, who was seventeen, and a native to San Antonio (like Texas Tavern chile), were married. They lived in San Antonio for a year and a half. Jim became a Kirby vacuum salesman, selling vacuum cleaners door-to-door. In a lunch interview with Velma and Matt's wife, Molly, Velma recalled she and Jim had "many wonderful experiences" during their time in San Antonio. She followed this statement up with lively recollections of their life as a young couple: moving multiple times, Jim learning to hunt for their food out of necessity, and her learning to cook venison because that's what there was to eat. Times for the young Bullington couple were lean in the way of finances yet full of adventure and fun.

Meanwhile, Jim's knack for salesmanship was revealing itself in his vacuum sales work. Going through three suits a day and becoming a self-proclaimed expert at using the Kirby wand to fend off dogs, Jim became quite successful as a Kirby salesman. So successful, in fact, in 1961 he won a national salesmanship award and a 1961 Plymouth Valiant. Velma said she never saw that car.

"It was the only new car I ever owned and I never even saw it," she told me, and laughed. Then she added, "Jim was so good at sales, he could sell something before he ever had it in his hands." Case in point: Jim sold the Valiant before he ever got it home. He used the money to make their mortgage payment. As far as Velma was concerned, that was just fine.

Shortly after winning the sales award, Jim was offered a Kirby distributorship to operate back in Roanoke. Velma said the idea of moving to Roanoke was exciting to her. She'd never lived outside of San Antonio or seen much outside her hometown, for that matter. It was daunting, too. Velma would be 1,400 miles from all she'd ever known. She also understood once they moved it would be incredibly difficult for her family to come visit her, and vice versa. Besides this, they owned a home that would need to be sold in a short period of time. Despite these obstacles, Jim and Velma knew the opportunity in Roanoke was one they would not pass on. They sold their home, said goodbye to Velma's family—hard for Jim, too, as he had developed a close relationship with Velma's dad—and in 1961, the couple moved to Roanoke.

Jim kept the Kirby distributorship in Roanoke for a year and a half. Then, at the coaxing of his older brother, Fred, Jim decided to move into the real estate market. Though it was Jim's name on the listings, selling real estate was a team effort between him and Velma. Velma did all the behind-the-scenes work: calling potential customers, making appointments, scheduling showings, and staging properties. Jim showed the properties and handled the sales.

The couple continued on this path for several years. Then, in 1967, two things seemed to providentially happen at the same time: the real estate market took a hit, and J. G.'s health deteriorated to the point he couldn't operate the Texas Tavern anymore. It was at this convergence Jim turned to consider—possibly for the first time—his place at the Texas Tavern.

In a *Roanoke Times* article dated February 11, 1980, celebrating the Texas Tavern's fiftieth anniversary, Jim, then forty-two, reflected on his entrance to the Tavern.

"I knew if anything happened to my dad, I'd have to do something with the Tavern," he told *Times* reporter Joe Kennedy.

Velma remembered it similarly. She recounted it in the same way she recounted many of her life's adventures with Jim. There was the idea, then there was Jim going all in after it, figuring it out as he went along.

"Pawpaw [J. G.] couldn't work anymore and needed to do something with the T.T.," said Velma. "Fred wasn't interested at all. Jim said, 'What the hey, I'll just see.'" Velma shrugged her shoulders and grinned at the memory; another day in the life with Jim Bullington.

In truth, the Texas Tavern didn't just need someone to take it over. It needed someone to keep it thriving into the next generation. The thirty-seven-year-old institution was truly beloved by two generations of Roanokers, going on three. However, for the last eight years, J. G. had closed the night shift. And while he worked at keeping the Tavern viable through his quirky advertising, he didn't recognize how that advertising needed to do more to capture the hearts of the next generation. These things were beginning to take their toll. For three decades, J. G. had been an excel-

Jim during his "early days" at the Tavern.

lent steward of the Tavern, taking it from restaurant to icon. Yet, in order for it to keep its footing in a fast-changing cultural landscape, the Texas Tavern needed a fresh set of eyes. Jim recognized all this. He understood the importance of the Tavern's place within the community. He also knew, as an instinct, even, what was needed for the Tavern to flourish through the next generation.

And so, Jim began his grand Tavern experiment. With two small children at home and one on the way, Jim traded his $210 weekly income for $65 a week—a 70 percent pay cut. He worked for two weeks during daytime hours, learning the Tavern's intricacies. Then, at twenty-nine years of age, Jim went from never having worked behind the Texas Tavern's counter to opening back up and managing the night shift. Velma, who'd hoped to soon go back to working herself, instead became her husband's steady support. She took on Texas Tavern payroll, apron and hat laundering, pressing and mending, and any other task that required her efforts behind the scenes.

"That was something," recalled Velma. "[Jim] had to sleep during the day and I had two little kids in the house and was pregnant and trying to keep them quiet. Yes, that was something."

The young Bullington couple continued in this way for two and a half years.

Jim (left) with his daughter, Kathryn, Gordon Barbour, and Mark Tenney at the Tavern's 60th Anniversary, 1990.

✪✪✪✪✪✪✪✪✪✪✪✪✪✪✪

When Jim opened the Tavern's night shift back up, there was only one other spot in downtown Roanoke open twenty-four hours. It was a place with a somewhat seedy reputation called the Tottle House. With the Tavern open once again, people now had options. This made after-hours at the Tavern quite interesting. On one of the Tavern's first nights being open twenty-four hours, Jim put twenty-three people in jail. After that, he began hiring off-duty police officers to hang out at the Tavern during nighttime hours. "I want my employees selling hamburgers," Jim used to quip. "I don't want them fightin' in the parking lot."

By the time Jim took over management of the Texas Tavern, it had become a Roanoke household name. From Nick's entrepreneurial spirit that sought being at the forefront of America's restaurant scene, to J. G.'s uncompromising stewardship of keeping fixed what wasn't broken, Jim had inherited a restaurant well established in the hearts and stomachs of its community. This in no way made Jim's job any easier. In fact, the very things that made the Tavern a popular food joint were some of Jim's greatest challenges. How does an old place like the Tavern become attractive to the "super-size me" generation? How does a hole-in-the-wall compete with big-box stores and chain everything? And what about the hollowing out of downtowns across America? In 1967, Roanoke's downtown was a hive of economic activity. Daytime foot traffic was immense. But the winds of change for urban America were about to sweep through. Over the next several decades, centers of commerce would flee their downtown hubs for more spacious and sprawling suburban pastures. Roanoke would not be exempt.

"It's the challenge any business [of longevity] faces," explained Matt one late fall afternoon as he and I looked through old Tavern photos. "Do you adapt and change to fit the current culture? Do you stay the same and wither? Or do you stay the same and thrive?"

Jim knew there was only one way for the Texas Tavern. He would keep it the same and make it thrive.

Beyond opening back up the night shift, Jim made two significant structural changes within months of coming to work at the Tavern. First, he replaced the old wooden front door with the glass door still there today. Second, he added air conditioning. Both changes set J. G. ablaze.

"Dad waited until my grandpa went to the farm [in Paris, Illinois] for a weekend, then he changed out the door," said Matt. "That old door was always breaking and it didn't look nice anymore. Dad always knew what made the Tavern successful. He wanted to keep the Tavern as it is. But there comes a time when practicality takes over." Matt paused and then laughed before continuing. "But my grandpa flipped his lid when he came back to the new door."

It was the same with the air conditioning. J. G. insisted air conditioning couldn't be retrofitted to the 1930s-era building. Jim insisted it absolutely could, and, furthermore, it had to be done if they were to stay viable. All across America, homes and businesses were being retrofitted and built with air-conditioning units. Folks would not long-suffer eating somewhere not equipped with it. Especially at a place like the Tavern, where the griddle kept the ten-stool restaurant uncomfortably toasty in warmer months and getting a cross-breeze was near impossible. Still, J. G. was unmoved by his son's reasoning. Likewise, Jim was unmoved by his father's belligerence. Shortly after the glass door went in, so did the air conditioning. Two generations later, Tavern goers don't know their beloved restaurant any other way.

As each decade passed, more and more businesses made their way from downtown Roanoke to the burgeoning suburbs, or else moved away all together. Crossroads Mall—the first indoor mall to open in Virginia—opened in 1961 on the north side of Roanoke. Twelve years later, Tanglewood Mall opened south of downtown. Then Valley View Mall opened in 1985. With each mall opening, Roanoke's retail landscape shifted further and further from downtown. And yet, in the face of all these complicating factors, the Texas Tavern grew busier than ever.

Several factors play into this. To begin with, the shifting economic scene for cities across America happened gradually, over decades. And while retail commerce shifted, other businesses in downtown Roanoke did not. Matt said he remembers when, even into the late 1980s and early 1990s, there was a plethora of foot traffic downtown. There was no shortage of folks on lunch breaks coming to the Tavern for a good, quick, and satisfying midday meal. Finally, Jim reopening the Texas Tavern's night shift was critical to keeping the Tavern thriving through his decades of ownership. While daytime businesses may have been slowly exiting downtown, nighttime establishments certainly were not. The City Market area—now full of fun, independently owned eateries— during Jim's era of ownership was full of raucous establishments open until 2 A.M., after which the Texas Tavern would do some of its best work: the work of "sobering up the city," as Jim liked to quip.

One of the most important changes Jim made for the Texas Tavern during his ownership was something Tavern goers never noticed. It was a critical move, however, for the restaurant's stability into the next generation. Since its beginning, the Bullingtons never owned the tiny scratch of land upon which Nick built the Tavern. They owned the building, but the land was still owned by the Thurman family. For years this land lease operated on nothing more formal than an annual handshake. Eventually, J. G. had the lease put into writing, but it remained an annual contract. When Jim came into Texas Tavern ownership, he recognized the increasing precariousness of this leasing situation. He negotiated a five-year lease with the owners, giving the Tavern some breathing room between lease renewals. He also began a series of attempts to purchase the land and secure the Tavern's location on Church Avenue.

The Thurman family had other plans, however. They had no intention of selling the property. They were happy to continue collecting a rent check from the Bullingtons for time eternal and assumed the Bullingtons would never think of moving their tiny restaurant, which had established itself so happily on their tiny stamp of real estate. They assumed wrong.

In 1983, after yet another rejected offer, Jim decided to call the owners' bluff. The Bullingtons still owned the lot further up on Church Avenue near the YMCA. It was the lot Nick bought decades earlier when he moved to Roanoke. The house was no longer erect, but the garage still existed, acting as a storage unit and convenient hiding place for the Bullington children's Christmas presents. Jim went to the owners one last time with an ultimatum: sell the land the Texas Tavern is built on, or we'll move our tiny restaurant up the street to that old property we already own. That was it. The owners acquiesced, knowing they could never do anything viable with the lot if the Tavern moved. After fifty-three years in existence, the Texas Tavern finally owned the land upon which it was built.

By the late 1980s, Jim was ready to expand the Texas Tavern's reach. While he wanted the Tavern itself to remain small, he wanted its food to go places. Jim looked at the franchising model of the larger chain restaurants and wondered how he might replicate something similar for the Tavern on a smaller scale. He went to work finding a kitchen and then remodeling it to meet federal approval. He also had to alter the chile recipe, switching brands of some ingredients, for large-batch production. Velma said she remembers weeks of having three crockpots of chili going at the house all at the same time, each one containing a different brand of starch.

On November 2, 1988, Snappy's Convenience Stores began selling Texas Tavern chile. By the end of the year, they'd sold more than 1,181 gallons. The terrific success prompted Jim to seek more partnerships. In January, Stop In Food Stores started selling Tavern chile in fifteen of its stores. By August, Texas Tavern chile could be found in twenty-seven mini-marts and convenience stores across the state of Virginia.

Chile advertisement for the wholesale business.

At the height of the wholesale service, the Bullingtons were delivering chile to seventy-five stores. Because the chile was delivered in its premade condition—concentrate, beans, and starch all separate—and needed to be made into batches on-site, product consistency became a concern. The Bullingtons and their employees were no longer in control. It was incumbent upon the convenience stores to prep the chile correctly. While there were many locations where the chile sold well, there were those that did not. Because of this, Jim decided to close the Tavern's wholesale operation. It was a worthwhile experiment lasting about eight years, and one Jim was fine with letting go in the end.

✪ ✪ ✪ ✪ ✪ ✪ ✪ ✪ ✪ ✪ ✪ ✪ ✪ ✪ ✪ ✪

With a majority of independently owned restaurants not making it past the five-year mark, and in an era when chain restaurants, both fast food and sit-down, were exploding across the country, the Texas Tavern was most definitely unique. And yet this didn't make its future secure. The industrial and commercial landscape of modern America continued shifting like fault lines, helping along the ripples of suburban sprawl.

Jim knew he couldn't rest on the Tavern's historic laurels. Times were a-changin'. While Nick and J. G. both made quirky advertising a central aspect of the Texas Tavern's identity, Jim took Tavern advertising to an entirely new level. He continued to build upon the quirkiness his father and grandfather had established. But he did something else, too. Jim took the Texas Tavern to cultlike status.

"My dad understood guerrilla marketing before it was ever a thing," said Matt in recounting his father's excellent and unique stewardship of the Tavern. In our late-modern era of tribalism and gluttonous social media marketing, it may be hard to appreciate how cutting edge Jim Bullington's approach to building and securing a loyal customer following truly was. But in the 1970s through the 1990s, when traditional outlets for advertising still reigned, the idea of reaching the masses one customer at a time was outlandish.

In a guerrilla-marketing strategy, unconventional and low-cost means are utilized to reach one's potential customer base. Jay Conrad Levinson coined the term in his 1984 book, *Guerrilla Advertising*. Levinson borrowed the term from guerrilla warfare, an irregular style of warfare utilizing tactical strategies such as sabotage, ambush, raids, and other elements of surprise, often employed by bands of armed citizens. In guerrilla marketing the same idea applies only without the violent animosity or bloodshed: take the customer by surprise, make an indelible impression, and create lots of social buzz. This is what Jim did in spades.

One example of Jim's guerilla marketing was beginning the sale of Tavern merchandise. He had three t-shirt designs created. Two of them would change with time and occasion, but the classic gold Texas Tavern t-shirt would—just as the Tavern itself—forever stay the same. He sold ball caps and handed out calendar magnets. His merchandise was cheap. This way people were more likely to buy it and become Texas Tavern walking billboard signs.Of course, Jim continued the Tavern's tradition of advertising through humor. This was as much within his genetic makeup as it was intentional. By now, Texas Tavern humor was even more quirky and unique. It had an old-timey feel to it—a nostalgia and innocence quickly being swallowed up and spit out by Vietnam, disco balls, and Watergate. Maybe the funny sayings gracing the Tavern walls were peculiar back in 1930 when the Tavern first opened. But by the 1970s and '80s, oddities such as "We don't cash checks or play with bumble bees" and "We serve buttermilk in a glass big enough to drown a small horse" sounded strange in the era of free love and rock 'n' roll. Jim recognized this and played it up, making it even more a part of the Tavern's identity.

But the most brilliant marketing strategy Jim employed through his decades of ownership was to make public what everyone already knew: the Texas Tavern was more than a place to get a burger, hot dog, and some strangely spelled chili. It was a place of history. It was a place of story. It was the story of a community where everyone was handed a leading role. Everyone contributed to the ongoing narrative, whether they meant to or not.

It was an angle Jim had afforded to him his father and grandfather did not. In fact, it was because of what his grandfather and father had done with the Tavern that made it so media-appealing by the time Jim stepped into ownership. When Nick opened the Tavern in 1930, he was busy capitalizing on America's newest innovations and ensuing trends related to standardization and America's shifting eating habits. Then J. G. took over and stewarded the restaurant, not fixing what wasn't broken and preserving what his father had started, partly because he hated change, but mostly out of his vision for the special place the Tavern was becoming. By Jim's era, the Texas Tavern had become its own living legend. It was the story of sinners and saints, millionaires and hobos, and all manner of folks in between. It was the story of late-night holdups and early-morning cups of joe. It was a story of decades and of days. Jim took all of it to the press.

For Jim, everything that happened in and around the Tavern became fodder for a story. Good, bad, or ugly, Jim used his quick wit and easy quips to draw the community in with its own narrative. The big University of Virginia versus Virginia Tech matchup one year became a publicity stunt that involved Jim making a bet with Bob Bersch, a local lawyer and faithful customer of the Tavern. If Virginia Tech won the game, Bersch would have to work behind the Tavern counter for the day. Virginia Tech won, and Bersch took his lickin' behind the counter. The *Roanoke Times* was there to capture the affair.

"That's got to be like Chinese water torture for a lawyer to be that close to money and not touch it," Jim teased to the *Times* reporter in front of his friend of twenty-five years. "That's why he's here, to increase the reputation of the legal profession by showing people he can do an honest day's work."

There was also the time the Tavern's security camera caught a robber who broke into the Tavern on Christmas—the only day the Tavern is closed. As he climbed over the counter, he revealed too much of his backside. This became a pithy story the local news dubbed the "Case of the Bare Bottomed Bandit." Jim turned it into an advertising opportunity in which he sought information and a $500 reward to anyone who could "crack the case." The infamous burglar came to be known inside Tavern walls as the "butt crack bandit."

The time Jim's mother, Libby, took a fall trying to get down from a Tavern stool turned into a joke about "the only sober person to fall down at the Tavern." It's still an oft-quoted line at the Tavern today.

Another genius of Jim's media marketing was his way of leaking a story to one part of the local media as a way to get them to jump on it and create buzz.

"Hey," he'd say to some local news reporter, "we have something big coming up, and I wouldn't want Channel 10 to get a jump on it." Said local reporter would agree he or she wouldn't want Channel 10 to get a jump on whatever the big thing was, either. It was a symbiotic relationship: the press got their story and the Texas Tavern got free publicity.

Another one of Jim's smart media moves was turning the Texas Tavern anniversary celebrations into annual newsworthy events. It wasn't that the Bullingtons never celebrated Tavern anniversaries before Jim. Old newspaper clippings show evidence of anniversary stories beginning with the Tavern's fortieth year in business. But the Tavern's fiftieth year in business caught the attention of the national media.

P.M. Magazine, a nationally syndicated evening television show with an entertainment news focus, ran a story on the Texas Tavern's fiftieth anniversary. The show used stories told by local reporters to fill their evening show with short pop-culture tidbits from across the country. In a nine-minute segment, Joel Kaczmarek, who also happened to be a neighbor to the Bullingtons, shared the "mystique" of the Texas Tavern with *P.M. Magazine* viewers across America. Jim was interviewed, as were customers of all ages—including two children who look to be all of six years old. Interspersed with interview clips were shots of employees preparing and serving Tavern fare along with customers rattling off orders and then eating the same food made the same way since the Depression. All this with Beethoven's *Ode to Joy* playing in the background.

Jim had a formula to the anniversary celebrations that Matt still follows today. Jim always involved the media and public officials in the celebration. He'd drop the price of hamburgers and hot dogs to an anniversary price: the year of the anniversary was the number of cents he'd charge for each item. For some of the bigger anniversary years, beginning with the fiftieth, Jim also commissioned local artist Eric Fitzpatrick, then a young fledgling artist trying to get a start, to paint Tavern scenes. Eric's style fit perfectly with the Texas Tavern. His paintings were rollicking, color-filled affairs, whimsical and full of both the hilarity and audacity considered normal at the Tavern. Eric always painted regular customers into the paintings. And just like the Renaissance artists, Eric would embed himself somewhere in the painting, too. Jim would unveil the print at the Tavern on anniversary day in front of the media and crowds of local folks. It was another one of Jim's symbiotic relationships: Jim helped Eric pay for college and launch his career as an artist. Eric helped Jim tell the Tavern's story in a colorful and visible way.

In all these ways, Jim took the Tavern's story to the public. Sure, he did it as a way to market the restaurant and keep its glass door open. But it was more than that. Jim believed in the power of the Texas Tavern's story. He knew the Tavern had become solid ground for the folks of Roanoke. In an era where most every aspect of life was becoming less and less personal—big-box stores, chain restaurants, name-brand everything—people craved places in their community they could point to as uniquely their own. Places that could never exist anywhere else on earth in the same way. In short, folks in Roanoke needed reasons to keep calling themselves Roanokers. The Texas Tavern had become one of those reasons, and an excellent one at that. Jim understood this. And he was determined to keep the Tavern's story alive, one customer, one bandit, one media stunt, and one anniversary celebration at a time.

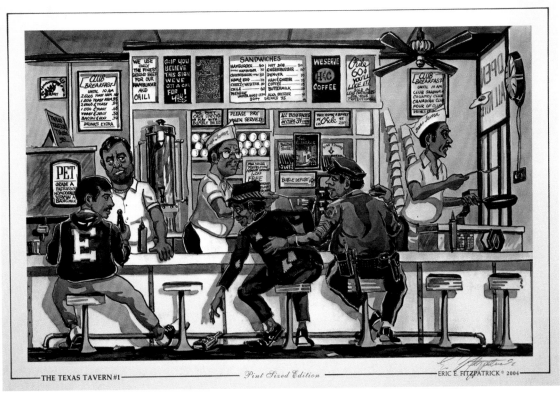

Eric Fitzpatrick's first commissioned painting for the Tavern.

To Jim, stewarding the Texas Tavern meant also stewarding its community. It was something he absorbed early in his bout with
polio, and also in watching his own father's familial care of employees.
Jim made it his vocation to help those down-and-outers of the community. He also was passionate in advocating for the lifeblood of the
community itself: Roanoke's downtown.

As from its beginning days, the Texas Tavern was—and still is—no
respecter of class, race, or social standing. Lawyers ate next to shift
workers who ate next to bankers who ate next to the homeless. Jim
made sure all were treated with the same dignity. He had an especially
soft spot for the less fortunate of the community.

Recreation of the grand opening photo for the Tavern's 50th Anniversary, 1980.

As mentioned earlier, Jim rubbed elbows with death a little too early in life. But he also had the quiet influence of his father's compassionate ways. For as much as the two butted heads in Jim's younger years, he absorbed J. G.'s own fondness for folks, especially for Tavern employees. From the very beginning as the Tavern's night manager, Jim was assimilating J. G.'s nuanced approach to always giving people the benefit of the doubt and always offering folks a hand-up when able.

Pete had been a Tavern grill man for J. G. for years. He was a loyal employee to a fault; and, sometimes it was a fault. Pete had some funny quirks about him, character traits that occasionally got in the way of a smooth-running operation. When Jim joined the Tavern management, it didn't take him long to notice Pete's quirks and get to wondering about Pete himself.

"Hey, what's the deal with that Pete guy?," Jim asked his father one day, soon after coming to work at the Tavern. J. G. immediately responded, but not in the expected way.

"Don't try to figure him out. You'll wind up in the funny farm," J. G. said to his son.

That was the end of that particular conversation. But the message to Jim was clear. Pete, as quirky and occasionally dysfunctional as he was, was also as faithful an employee as could be. This was worth more to J. G. than any frustrations his eccentricities could cause. From this conversation, a sort of grooming began—or perhaps continued with more intentionality than Jim had earlier recognized. It was the start of a generational training of father to son on the familial nature and civic mindedness of the Texas Tavern.

Jim would have ample opportunities through his years at the Tavern to offer a hand-up to faithful employees. There was Henry, who spent time in and out of jail for petty crimes. Jim always had a place for Henry behind the counter when he was on a good streak. And when Henry was on a bad streak Jim still looked after him. During one such streak, while serving time in jail, Henry received word that his mother was dying. Jim convinced Judge Fitzpatrick—Eric Fitzpatrick's father, regular customer and Jim's longtime friend—to let Henry out of jail long enough to go visit his mother one last time. Jim promised to take full responsibility for Henry. Jim drove Henry the several hours away to where his mother was hospitalized, waited in his car for many more hours while Henry sat with her, and then drove him home and deposited him safely back in jail. Jim was also known to send his employees with heart problems to local cardiologist Hayden Hollingsworth, who was also a close friend. Hollingsworth told a *Roanoke Times* reporter in a February 2015 article celebrating Jim's life, "He was always putting others' needs first. . . . I suspect when [his employees] were in the hospital, he picked up their bills for them."

Jim advocated for the down-and-outers of the community as well, even those who might seem—from the outside—intent on doing his Tavern harm. One night around midnight, a woman tried to hold up the Tavern with an unloaded .38 pistol. She didn't pull the gun out right away. First, she made her demand of $100 to grill man Mark Tenney. When Tenney ignored her, she pulled out the gun and tried again. Meanwhile, customers slid past her, found stools, ordered, and ate as if nothing was amiss. She asked Tenney one more time if he was going to give her the money. "Nah," said Tenney and kept flipping burgers. The woman left, despondent. Someone at the Tavern called the police. They easily found the woman and arrested her. When she went to trial, Jim Bullington showed up and pleaded with the prosecuting attorneys and judge. He asked that they enroll her in a mental health treatment program rather than give her jail time. "She doesn't need to be in jail," he insisted. "She needs help."

✪ ✪ ✪ ✪ ✪ ✪ ✪ ✪ ✪ ✪ ✪ ✪ ✪ ✪ ✪

Besides employees and those less fortunate in the community, Jim stood up for the life of downtown Roanoke. In 2001, the *Roanoke Times* wanted to expand their operation and build a large addition for a new printing press. The expansion project was met with blowback by a local property owner who'd recently built a set of apartment buildings close to where the expansion was to happen. He complained that the *Times*' new building would block residents' views. The city conducted a zoning hearing to settle the matter. Jim Bullington was the only downtown business owner to attend the meeting. Jim spoke vehemently on behalf of the *Times*. His argument was logical, impassioned, and fundamentally downtown focused. Matt, in his late twenties at the time, went with his father to the meeting. He still has his dad's words memorized:

"If you don't want to listen to jet noise, don't move next to the airport. If you don't want to smell goats then don't buy a house next to a goat farm. And if you don't want to see buildings, don't move downtown. Downtown is what it is. To impede the progress of the *Roanoke Times*, which is an institution down here, is something we cannot allow to happen. I shudder to think of a downtown that doesn't have the *Roanoke Times* in it."

The *Roanoke Times* won the day, thanks in large part to Jim's backing. "Texas Tavern always punches above its weight," Jim liked to say. It certainly did that day.

Jim remained a strong advocate for Roanoke's downtown throughout his career. Of course, he was concerned for the life of the Tavern. But he was also concerned for the life of his community. He knew the health of any town is measured by its downtown pulse. Jim was adamant about keeping Roanoke's pulse strong. It was a conviction he passed on to his son, Matt, who has followed his father's example in putting the Tavern's weight behind important downtown issues today.

✪ ✪ ✪ ✪ ✪ ✪ ✪ ✪ ✪ ✪ ✪ ✪ ✪ ✪ ✪

In the final minutes of the *P.M. Magazine's* fiftieth anniversary segment, there is an interview exchange I think best expresses Jim Bullington's ownership of the Texas Tavern. Jim is asked to speak to the

Texas Tavern's longevity and success. He answers carefully and with conviction. As he speaks, his presence fills the space around him. In his distinct southwest Virginia dialect and without stumbling over a single word, Jim Bullington says the following: "Simplicity, good people, and good fortune." He then pauses before continuing:

> By simplicity, I mean the original recipes were simple and we haven't changed them. We buy the best of everything and we leave everything alone. . . . The concept of the Tavern is simple. You give the customer the best you can for the money and give a fair shake to the customer.
>
> By good people, I mean we have good, loyal employees, and good, loyal customers. There is a friendliness between employees and customers. You don't get that overnight. It takes years to build.
>
> And good fortune speaks for itself. We've been fortunate over the years to deal with good people like this and we're grateful for it and we appreciate it. And I think in a nutshell maybe that wraps it up.

A Happy Birthday at the T.T.

I visited Texas Tavern following a night of music and drinks with friends for my twenty-fifth birthday. As I ordered my cheesy and bowl with, it came up that I had been celebrating. The lovely men behind the counter took a pinto bean and struck a match and stuck it in the bean for my T.T.-esque restaurant-style birthday cake, if you will. It was very special.

—Maddie Osterhaus, Roanoke

TAVERN EMPLOYEES THROUGH THE YEARS

"It always comes back to the employees behind the counter . . . there's so many moving parts, that's why it's so important to have good employees."

Matt Bullington
fourth-generation Texas Tavern owner

✪ ✪ ✪ ✪ ✪ ✪ ✪ ✪ ✪ ✪ ✪ ✪ ✪ ✪ ✪

I've never met a successful restaurant owner yet who doesn't nod straight his employees' way when asked what makes his or her restaurant a success. The Bullingtons are no exception. The following is a short list and description of some of the Tavern's longest-serving and most legendary employees.

Paul Starkey
Tavern manager 1934–1967

The first legendary T.T. employee was Paul Starkey, a hulk of a man who was known to palm the counter and jump over in one swift movement when an unruly customer needed help finding the door. Hired by Nick Bullington, Paul was with the Texas Tavern from only four years into the Roanoke Tavern's existence to the year Jim Bullington—third-generation Tavern owner—decided to make the Tavern his career. According to cousin David Bullington, Paul was the "law of the west." His size and strength alone made him a respectable figure among Roanokers. "He

Paul Starkey, ca. 1940.

was very well known," said David. "He worked back in the day when if you were going to cause trouble, Paul'd just throw you out—literally."

There is a funny story about Paul Starkey to illustrate this point: after a disagreement behind the counter, a disgruntled customer was trying to make his case to a Roanoke judge, claiming he was assaulted by Paul Starkey. The judge looked hard at the customer and said, "You're claiming Paul Starkey hit you? If Paul Starkey hit you yesterday, you'd be in the hospital today. Case dismissed."

Paul remained manager when J. G. came to take over Tavern operations, continuing on for another twenty-five years or more. He finally retired in the mid-1960s. Paul was the Tavern's manager through Jim's childhood but had retired by the time Jim came back to take over Texas Tavern ownership.

Gordon Barbour
Tavern manager 1968–1995

Gordon Barbour fell into Tavern management somewhat by accident. The Korean War veteran had been a Texas Tavern regular since he was a child. After he came back from serving in Korea in the early 1950s, Gordon took a job as a city firefighter. He would stop at the Tavern most mornings for a cup of coffee. On one of those mornings, J. G. offered Gordon a part-time position behind the counter. Gordon paused for a moment, then looked at J. G. and said, "Sure, I'll work."

Gordon worked at the Tavern part-time for years. In 1968, when J. G. retired and passed the torch to his son Jim, Gordon left his post as a city firefighter and took on full-time employment as the Texas Tavern's manager. He managed the Tavern throughout Jim's years of ownership and helped train Matt before retiring in 1995.

In a *Roanoke Times* article featuring Gordon's decades of Texas Tavern service and retirement announcement, Gordon waxed nostalgic about the changing times while he was with the T.T. From the first day he tied the Tavern apron around his waist, hamburgers had gone

Gordon Barbour (right) with Jim Bullington at Gordon's retirement, 1995.

from 15 cents to 95 cents. Beans came in twenty-five pound bags rather than fifty-pound ones. He navigated the tricky transition from the "no ketchup" to "ketchup grudgingly" policy and did it in true Tavern spirit. He also recalled the time in the 1960s when he was still working full-time as a firefighter and answered a call at his part-time job, the Texas Tavern. One of the employees accidentally set the back of the Tavern on fire while he was showing another employee—inside the restaurant— how to work the kerosene-fueled flame thrower J. G. had brought to the Tavern to melt ice on the front sidewalk. "The fire trucks arrived," recalled Gordon to *Roanoke Times* reporter Dan Casey. "All the help was standing outside. All the customers stayed inside. They were still eating. The firefighters had to run them out of here."

Dan Siler

Tavern employee 1955–2005

Dan Siler's time as a Texas Tavern grill man spanned three generations of Bullington ownership. He worked the grill at the Tavern for almost fifty years. Some customers had Dan cook for them from elementary school to near-retirement age. Dan was well known outside the Tavern as well. He helped coach baseball for many years and earned the name "Herb" after the 1950s major leaguer Herb Score.

Dan was thin as a rail and fast. Kids loved to go down to the T.T. and bet him to footraces in the Tavern's parking lot. Dan would happily oblige them. The kids usually lost. Dan, like Gordon Barbour, can be found in several of Eric Fitzpatrick's art prints commemorating Tavern anniversaries. The *Roanoke Times* even featured Dan's decades-long work as a Tavern grill man. Dan's dedication to the Tavern was something he was always proud of, and something the Bullingtons never took for granted.

Dan Siler, ca 1977. (Courtesy The Roanoker *magazine)*

Timothy Goff

Tavern employee 1988 to current manager

Timothy Goff began working at the Texas Tavern on June 12, 1988, when he was just sixteen years old. It wasn't behind the counter, however. Tim's first job at the Tavern was the unenviable task of scraping paint off the outside of the building, all fifty-plus layers of it. He did that job in a week. Jim Bullington was so impressed with Tim's work ethic, he offered him a job behind the counter. Tim started working days with Dan Siler and Gordon Barbour. In 1990, he switched to the night shift. In May of 1993, Tim became night manager and worked for five years in this position. In April of 1999, the Bullingtons pulled him

*Timothy Goff on the grill during the Tavern's 80th Anniversary celebration.
(Don Petersen)*

from the night shift and began grooming him to manage the day-to-day operations as Paul Starkey and Gordon Barbour had before him. He even has the prestigious job of making the Texas Tavern's famous chile in its concentrate form several times a week. Tim has been serving as assistant general manager and Matt Bullington's "right hand man" for the entirety of Matt's ownership of the Tavern.

Like the Tavern legends before him, Tim has played his part in a number of memorable Tavern stories. There was the time in 1993, while working the grill on the night shift, Tim had to tell a drunk and belligerent customer to leave after the man wouldn't stop harassing Tavern employees. The customer was so mad he went outside on the sidewalk, punched and shattered the grill window, then took off running. Two other customers—who happened to both be Marines in town on leave—chased after the man, caught him in the parking garage across the street, drug him back to the Tavern's parking lot, and pinned him down until the police arrived. There was also the time on the night shift Tim bet a customer $20 he couldn't drink a gallon of milk in an hour. The customer took him up on the challenge and gulped down his final glass of milk—eight large glasses in total—with five minutes to spare. The man won the money, but a week later he told Tim, "I felt so awful after drinking all that milk, I wouldn't do it again for $1,000." Finally, there was the time Carter Burgess—former assistant secretary of defense, president of TWA, ambassador to Argentina, and regular T.T. customer—tripped when walking into the Tavern one day. He fell into the cigarette machine, causing a gash on his head. Tim grabbed the medical kit and patched up the gash. Burgess was so appreciative, he left Tim a $5 tip after he ate.

Tim has been serving behind the Texas Tavern's counter for more than thirty years now. Though he has the day-to-day managerial duties to look after, Tim still works the grill regularly. He is one of the fastest grill men to ever work at the Texas Tavern.

From left to right: long-time Tavern employees Cecil Spradin, Tim Goff, and Randy Dodd. (Molly Bullington)

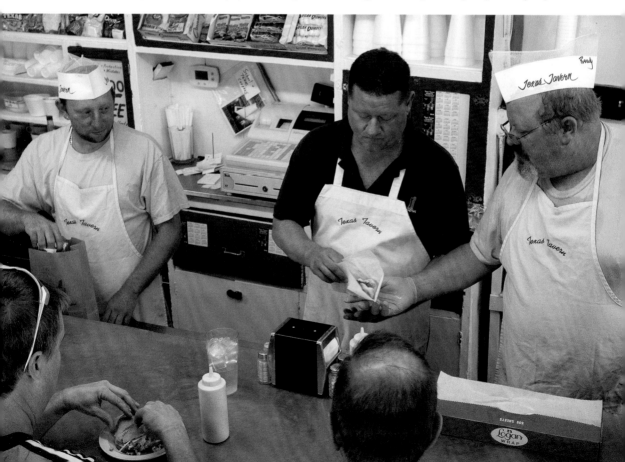

The Tavern at Daybreak

"You're gonna stay at the Tavern until the morning, aren't ya?" the young inebriated man said to me between bites of his cheesy.

"Why? What happens in the morning?" I asked, wondering what secret Tavern time I had yet to discover.

"Who knows? Everyone's asleep!"

That exchange prompted my early-morning visit to the Tavern. The city was still asleep as I made my way downtown. Church Avenue was a corridor layered in silence and shadows except for the Tavern's neon EAT sign, lit like a beacon for the wandering and the weary. I walked through the Tavern's open door, sat down on stool number four, and made myself at home.

During the two hours I was there, no more than seven folks stopped in, all of them regular customers. Cecil often had their coffee or juice waiting and their order going on the grill before they sat down. There was the usual small talk, long stretches of silence, and much sharing of the day's paper. I ordered an egg, bacon, and cheese sandwich on an English muffin. Cecil slathered each side of my toasted muffin with melted butter before putting it together. I ate slow, appreciating every bite and the quiet around me. Gradually, the morning sun lit through the Tavern's windows, saturating everything in its golden glow. Even Cecil's face took on its warmth as he looked out the window. His head was tilted in a way suggesting he did this every morning.

"I guess I'm pretty lucky," he said, his tone full of quiet reverence. "I get to watch the sun come up every day. Not many people get to say that."

Roanoke's Melting Pot

Young, old, rich, poor, blue collars mingle with white collars and the greasy and the suited rub elbows at Roanoke's legendary Texas Tavern, where lines have been known to stretch for blocks as patrons wait their turn at the specialty of the house — a 50-cent bowl of chili. The TT, in its 47th year at the same location, is owned by Jim Bullington, third generation proprietor of the little restaurant that has more employees (12) than seats (10). Gordon Barbour is current manager. His son Steve cleans up below (left) as Dan Siler stops to catch his breath (below right).

Photo Essay By Tom Porter

Photo essay featured in The Roanoker *magazine. (Courtesy* The Roanoker)

IVES AND
CASEY COLUMNS

*"On Saturday night the Tavern is a ritual, mainly
because my old lady always develops an unnatural craving
for a Cheesy Western around about one o'clock in the morning."*

Mike Ives

in his *Roanoke Times* column, 1975

"Texas Tavern, let's have some chile and make up."

Dan Casey

from his eighty-first Tavern birthday column

✪ ✪ ✪ ✪ ✪ ✪ ✪ ✪ ✪ ✪ ✪ ✪ ✪ ✪ ✪

Over decades, the Texas Tavern slowly made the transformation from burger joint to a kind of church. One thing spurring on its change was the regular amount of press it received from local journalists. In particular, two *Roanoke Times* columnists, Mike Ives and Dan Casey, wrote—and in Casey's case, still writes—about the Tavern in a way that gave credence to the idea the Tavern is more than a restaurant.

But they did it in very different ways.

Mike Ives wrote for the *Roanoke Times* in the 1960s and 1970s. He wrote a regular column that had a sort of *Cheers* feel about it: local guy who prattles on about local things that don't appear to amount to much. Except by the end of each column the reader feels a little more connected to his or her hometown.

Mike Ives loved the Texas Tavern. He was a regular customer, and the Tavern often showed up in his articles as a natural extension of his personhood, not unlike a parent talking about his kids. Even when Mike's column had nothing to do with the Tavern, somehow the Tavern managed to show up. There was the time he wrote about other food joints in Roanoke where one could get some good cheap eats. He started the column with a joke about the grill man at the Tavern being sore with him. According to the grill man, Ives's perpetual writing about the cheesy western in his columns was making the grill man's job harder. There was another time Ives wrote about how he couldn't think of anything to write about that day. The column ended up being about nothing except that he was primed to write about something marvelous after having fueled his brain on Tavern food. Whether Ives wrote about the Texas Tavern overtly or slid in a reference sideways, it was clear he was writing from the inside out; the Tavern as an extension of himself and his everyday life.

Dan Casey is the current columnist for the *Roanoke Times*. Like Mike Ives, Casey writes about local things, or how national things affect Roanokers. He writes in a sort of gossipy, tongue-in-cheek manner. One can never tell with Casey when he's being serious and when he's not. Sometimes this gets him in trouble.

For the Texas Tavern's eightieth anniversary in 2010, Casey wrote the first of what has become an annual Texas Tavern birthday tribute. He wrote about how much he likes the idea of the Tavern: how it's withstood change despite the changing times around it, how it stands for all folks no matter who they are, and how it's become a local legend of sorts. Then he went on to write several more paragraphs about how he didn't like their food.

This was a bad idea. I wonder if any other article Dan Casey's written has elicited so heated a response. On both sides.

Many of Casey's responders took him to task for disparaging the Texas Tavern's food, especially on its birthday. They spoke of the generous nature of the Bullington family, the Tavern's solid and dependable nature within the community, and the simple fact that nobody cares if Casey doesn't like the Tavern's food. Jim Bullington, five years into his Tavern retirement, was quick and—as expected—masterful in his response. "Some people don't like my food," he wrote in an email rebuttal to Casey, "but no one likes your newspaper."

However, there were those who praised Casey for saying out loud what many people were scared to utter, even behind closed doors. These people did *not* think the Texas Tavern's food was good. They couldn't understand what the fuss was about. What was so great about an outdated, ten-stool restaurant that serves thin-patty hamburgers without ketchup or tomatoes, and chili full of beans?

There, at the center of the swirling opinions, stood the eighty-year-old Texas Tavern, faithfully serving its chile and cheesy westerns by the thousands, ten at a time. As many of the responders suggested, the Texas Tavern is not a place that can be known by slicing it into pieces and seeing it as only under a microscope. This would be like conducting an autopsy on a person to try and understand what made him weep or laugh or be filled with contentment. No living thing can be fully known in this way. No tree's life-giving shade can be known by studying its rings. No bird's lilting song can be heard by examining its vocal chords. And no amount of comfort and wholeness of the Tavern's place can be discerned by noting the amount of beans in its chile or the thinness of its patties.

Casey realized his error and backtracked his criticisms. In his next column, Casey candidly wrote about the deluge of responses he'd received from both sides of the aisle. On the Tavern's eighty-first anniversary, he wrote a column that poked fun at the serious response over his disparaging column the year before. He then offered an apology of sorts. He made glowing—meaning satirical and funny—remarks on the Tavern's chile, extolling its virtues for plugging radiator leaks, as plaster, and calling it the best chili on two continents. The Bullingtons forgave Casey, which surprised to no one. Jim and Casey even grew to have a deep and abiding respect for one another. So much so, that when Jim was in his final weeks of life at Carilion Hospital, Casey went to visit him. And every year since the infamous eightieth-anniversary column, Casey has written a lively column to celebrate, always weaving tall tale together with truth, serving only to grow the legend that is the Texas Tavern.

Ives and Casey wrote from opposite perspectives on the Tavern. Ives knew the Tavern from the inside out. He frequented the Tavern so often the grill man would start cooking his order before he ever spoke a word. Casey, on the other hand, came into his knowing the Tavern from the outside in. He recognized the Texas Tavern's revered position within the community and could understand why from the facts. But he didn't know it as a regular customer. He didn't like Tavern food and was taken to task for making his opinion public. Casey could have easily chosen to never write about the Texas Tavern again. But he didn't do that. Instead, he found a new way—his own unique way—of making the Texas Tavern *his* Tavern, too.

Ives's and Casey's columns reveal yet another reason the Texas Tavern has become more than just a restaurant. The Tavern allows itself to be amenable and meaningful to each and every person desiring to engage with it, whether from the inside out or outside in. It meets each one without judgment, day or night, without compromising its own character in the process.

All it asks in return is that you check your status at the door.

Building Bonds at the T.T.

Back in 2001, when my mom first started dating my stepdad, Wayne, all I knew about him was that he loved James Bond and Roanoke. The first mutual interest we discovered was music and sound engineering. I was learning to run a stage show with my dad's local cover band, while Wayne was running the stage show for our church. Eventually, I started helping Wayne at church.

One summer night in 2002 after church, Wayne asked if I'd ever been to Texas Tavern. I said no, but I'd heard of it. He was aghast that anyone born in Roanoke could make it to nearly teenage-years (I'd just turned twelve) without having sat down at that bar. So, we went there for dinner before heading home.

I distinctly remember Wayne ordering a cheesy with, a bowl with, and a glass of buttermilk. Then he ordered for me the first two, of what now surely number in the thousands, "hots, just chili" I've eaten there.

We talked about Roanoke, its history, his history here, and what it meant to him to grow up and raise a family in this town he loved. Wayne and I developed a great connection that night. I consider him just as much a part of my family as any blood relatives.

Since then, I've had the good fortune of introducing younger friends and family to the T.T. And I always think about how something as simple as cheap and delicious food could create such a lasting and important family memory.

—Chris Deason, Roanoke

ADVERTISING ACROSS THE GENERATIONS

*"These guys do a great job of branding and with media.
There is great stewardship. They have a gene for advertising."*
David Bullington
cousin to Matt Bullington

✪ ✪ ✪ ✪ ✪ ✪ ✪ ✪ ✪ ✪ ✪ ✪ ✪ ✪ ✪

From its beginning, advertising has always been Texas Tavern's second specialty. Nick kicked it off with his catchy signs and funny advertising bills he'd hand out or post in the newspaper. J. G. continued the trend. He had an especially smooth and witty—*wicked smart*, as his grandson, David Bullington, called it—way with the pen. Jim took Texas Tavern advertising to an entirely new level. With his guerilla marketing tactics and foresight to turn every situation into a media-worthy event, Jim took the already storied restaurant and turned it into a living legend. Matt continues the Tavern's legacy, navigating it safely through the advertising turbulence of the twenty-first century.

The following pages include some highlights of Texas Tavern advertising through the generations.

Nick Bullington
1930–1938

NOTICE!
Come on back business
All Is Forgiven!

Texas Tavern
114 Church Avenue, S. W.

DELIGHTFUL
FOOD
At Stock Market Prices

Food served here is the
BEST Quality that can be
Purchased. None better can
be had at any eating place
at any price.

*Give the Lady and the cook
stove a rest*
Take home a Sack of Hamburgers
A Pint of Chili.
Cost 20c for Each Person

DeLuxe Hot Ham, Cheese, or
Egg Sandwich, 10 cents

We Seat 1,000 People
Ten at a Time

TEXAS
TAVERN
114 Church Ave. S. W.
*A Classy Little Sand-
wiche Shop*
Morning, Noon, Nite After
Theatre, After The Dance

5c Hamburgers
TAKE HOME A SACK

Three Special Sand
10c
Ham & Egg, W
Denver

10c – Mexican Ch

Creamed Butter
Frozen Mu
Free Parking Wh
Trade In That Frown
Open Day

Parking Space
For Rent
25c a Day – $3.00 per Mo.

Texas Tavern
114 W. CHURCH AVE.
Clean, Dry Lot

5c-Hamburger-5c
Buy 'Em By the Sack

Chile, Spaghetti,
De Luxe Sandwiche
Open All Night
Weather Forecast
Chile Today And Chile Tomorrow

J. G. Bullington
1938–1967

Texas Tavern—2x2—Times, April 30

聯合則強 / 聯合必勝

TEXAS TAVERN
114 W. Church Ave.
Announces
The Opening of the Newest
Texas Tavern
95 5-Chome, Hachiman-Dori, Fukiai-Ku
Kobe, Japan
Under personal supervision of Mr. Harold (Hickey) Woods,
formerly of Woods Bros. Coffee Co. of Roanoke, Va.
We cordially invite all our old friends and customers to
visit the newest TEXAS TAVERN on your next trip to Kobe.

TEXAS TAVERN
Lynchburg   ROANOKE   Kobe

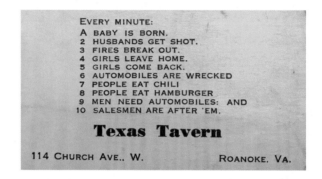

EVERY MINUTE:
A BABY IS BORN.
2 HUSBANDS GET SHOT.
3 FIRES BREAK OUT.
4 GIRLS LEAVE HOME.
5 GIRLS COME BACK.
6 AUTOMOBILES ARE WRECKED
7 PEOPLE EAT CHILI
8 PEOPLE EAT HAMBURGER
9 MEN NEED AUTOMOBILES: AND
10 SALESMEN ARE AFTER 'EM.

Texas Tavern

114 CHURCH AVE., W.   ROANOKE, VA.

TRIAKAIDEKAPHOBIA
(Mental fear of the number 13)

- Texas Tavern -

611 MAIN STREET
Good For One Hamburger Sandwich
Wed. March 13th --- Thurs. March 14th
"13 is our Lucky Number."

Jim Bullington
1967–2005

BREAKFAST
2 Eggs, Meat, Toast, Jelly,
LEGAL ADVICE,
MARRIAGE COUNSELING
and REAL
ESTATE
APPRAISALS **$1.90**

Texas Tavern
In Beautiful, Historic
Downtown Roanoke
Always Open

VOTED - BEST
"Hotdog"
"Inexepensive Lunch"
"Late Night Dinner"
As Chosen by Readers of
The Roanoker Magazine
Thanks!!!

Texas Tavern
In Beautiful Historic
Downtown Roanoke
Always Open

**Sandwich of
Champions**

CHEEZY WESTERN
Only At

Texas Tavern
In Beautiful, Historic
Downtown Roanoke
Always Open

**Thanks
Roanoke
For
68 YEARS**
Fri., Feb. 13, 1930
to
Fri., Feb. 13, 1998

Texas Tavern
In Beautiful Historic
Downtown Roanoke
Always Open

Matt Bullington
2005–present

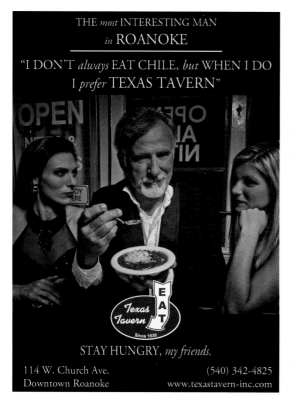

THE *most* INTERESTING MAN
in ROANOKE

"I DON'T *always* EAT CHILE, *but* WHEN I DO
I *prefer* TEXAS TAVERN"

STAY HUNGRY, *my friends.*

114 W. Church Ave.
Downtown Roanoke

(540) 342-4825
www.texastavern-inc.com

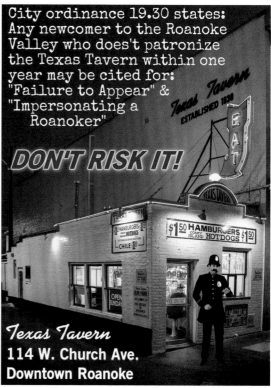

City ordinance 19.30 states:
Any newcomer to the Roanoke
Valley who does't patronize
the Texas Tavern within one
year may be cited for:
"Failure to Appear" &
"Impersonating a
Roanoker"

DON'T RISK IT!

Texas Tavern
114 W. Church Ave.
Downtown Roanoke

You Never Know Where the Tavern Will Show Up

In 2002, I'd been in Roanoke nearly a year. I made some friends who introduced me to Texas Tavern in the same late-night manner a lot of people get introduced: at 2 A.M. when the bars are closing. I was an instant fan.

On a scuba diving trip that year, the local dive shop coordinated a bus trip to Florida and I happened to be riding with this couple. It was the middle of the night. After we'd become acquainted, I made the comment—somewhere around 2 A.M., I think—"I could go for a bowl with and a cheesy western." The couple laughed and the man said, "That's funny, do you know who I am?" And I, of course, had no clue.

It was Matt Bullington and his girlfriend, now wife, Molly. We've been friends ever since.

—Mike Miller, Roanoke

In 1997, while on a long vacation to Nova Scotia, Jim and Velma Bullington met a gentleman while touring about one day. They struck up a conversation in which the man asked where the Bullingtons called home. "Roanoke, Virginia," said Jim. "Oh," replied the man, "I've been to Roanoke before. Have you ever heard of a place called the Texas Tavern?" "Yeah," said Jim. "I own it."

—Story retold by Matt Bullington

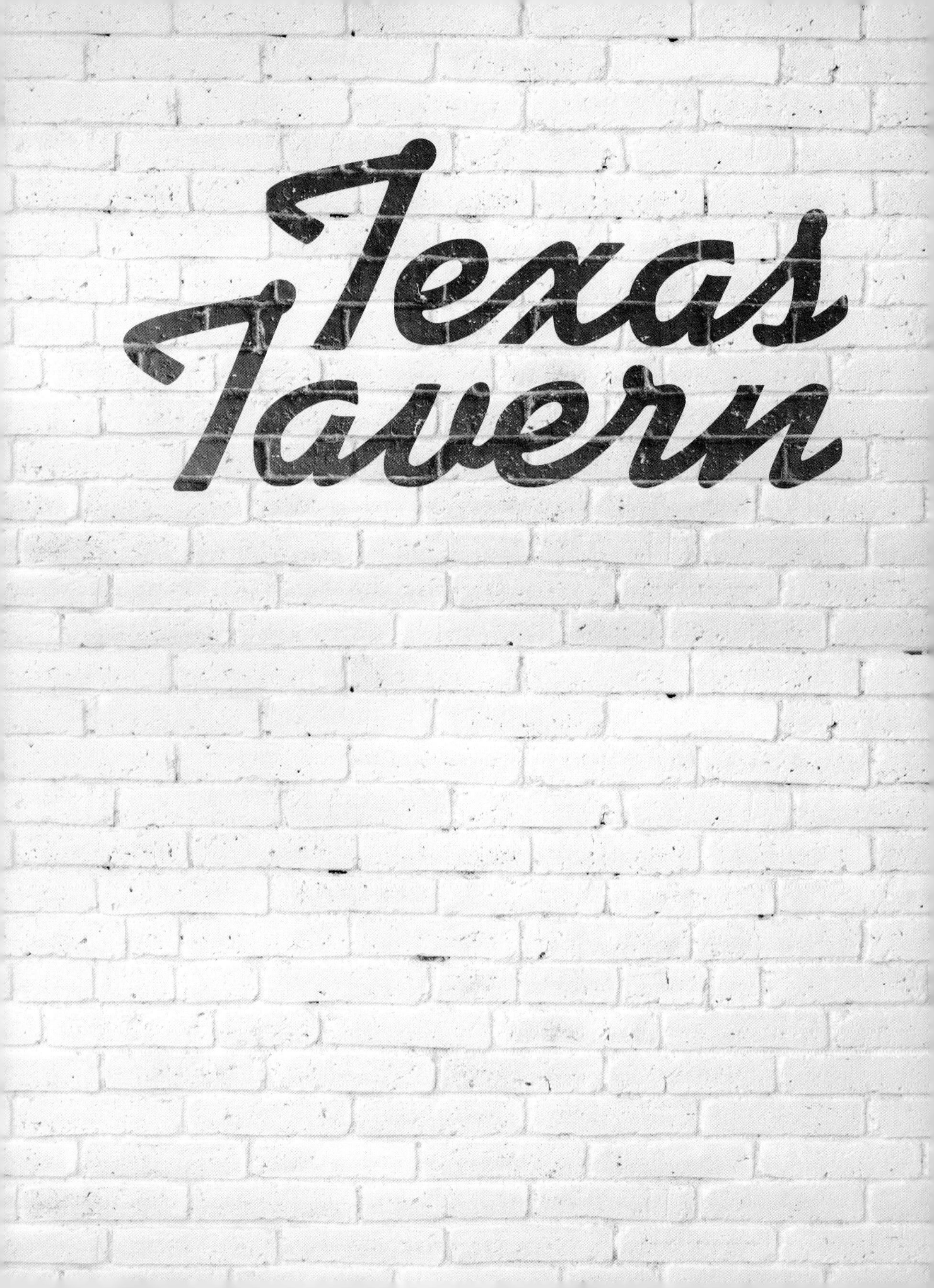
Texas
Tavern

4TH GEN

MATT BULLINGTON

Nothing in this world takes the place of persistence.

PRESIDENT CALVIN COOLIDGE

Matt Bullington, fourth generation Texas Tavern owner. (Molly Bullington)

The Texas Tavern's fourth generation of Bullington ownership came into the world on March 23, 1974. James Matthew Bullington was the fourth and youngest of Jim and Velma's children. He was also their only son. By the time Matt was born, Jim had been operating the Tavern for seven years. The year Matt turned four, the Tavern turned fifty. From packing crackers while watching Tom and Jerry on Saturday mornings to eating his dinner in the Tavern's back kitchen as a toddler, Matt's world was never one without the Tavern in it. And yet Matt didn't think much about the Tavern day-to-day. It was a part of his life—neat to be able to offer Texas Tavern hot dogs and hamburgers when his buddies would come over—but not something he thought about otherwise. Like his father, Matt never worked at the Tavern until he was considering it as a career.

Instead, Matt grew up playing sports, collecting baseball cards, and building a healthy-sized lawn mowing business. He knew the only way he would get his own car was if he bought it himself. So, when he turned thirteen, Matt borrowed money from his father for a new lawn mower. Jim agreed to cover half the cost of the mower if Matt would also keep the family yard mowed. By the time he was in high school, Matt was caring for twenty lawns in his South County neighborhood. He remembers having to push his lawn mower up Sugar Loaf Mountain Road in order to get to some of his clients' homes. But it was worth it. Matt paid for his first car in cash, something he took great pride in. And like the Bullington men before him, Matt still has his notebook with all the names of his clients and the dates he cut their lawn.

After high school, Matt went to Virginia Western for three semesters, then transferred to Roanoke College. He didn't consider joining his dad in the family business until sometime during his junior year of college. Before then, he thought he wanted to be a lawyer. His dad had a fascination with law. According to Matt's mother, Velma, Jim had always wanted to study law. He would sometimes go to court and sit for hours, just to watch the justice system at work. There were also a lot of lawyers who came into the Tavern for lunch, and they were nice customers. But

Matt started noticing something about them. They often seemed weary. One day, while working behind the Tavern's counter, Matt received this single piece of insight from one such customer: "You know, there's a lot of ways to make a living," the man began. "This used to be nice. It's just not as nice as it used to be."

Matt considered the man's words with all sincerity. "You know," he said to me in recounting his process of deciding on the Tavern life, "people come into the Tavern and I give 'em a hot dog or a hamburger. They're happy. I get paid for it. I'm happy. They leave. Everyone's happy and has a nice day. No one's mad at the other for it 99 percent of the time."

With all this at play, coupled with his father's impending retirement, Matt shifted focus. He decided to pursue a business degree at Roanoke College. He also took up steady employment at the Texas Tavern starting with the night shift, just like his dad.

Matt's decision to carry on the Tavern mantle wasn't without its soul-searching, however. One of the agreements Matt and his father made included Matt learning the business then taking a couple years after college to travel. Matt loves to travel. Without a doubt—outside his family—experiencing other places and cultures is Matt's favorite thing. Jim valued travel for Matt, too. Jim had seen other parts of the world before landing back in Roanoke and pursuing the proverbial "settling down." Jim was happy to oblige Matt in his desire. All was well, the plan was in place. Then, in 1995, two years before Matt was scheduled to graduate college, Jim's long-time manager, Gordon Barbour, decided to retire.

Gordon's exit left Jim with several gap years in Tavern management. He trained another person to manage after Gordon, but it became clear this wasn't a long-term solution. It was a critical moment for Matt. He desperately wanted to spend some time between college and Tavern ownership to spread his wings. But fate wasn't having it. His dad was ready to move toward retirement. The current management situation post-Gordon wasn't tenable. Matt knew he didn't want the Tavern to go into different hands. Still, Matt had his time of wrestling fate. Of course,

Young Matt with his dad, Jim, behind the Tavern counter, 1995.

the Tavern came out on top. Once he made peace with his decision to move straight from college to the Tavern life, Matt Bullington was all in.

It's no surprise Matt's best instruction came from his dad. Early on, while Matt was still in college, Jim advised his son to go work at McDonald's for six months. Why? So he could understand the importance of systems.

"McDonald's is the master of systems," said Matt. "They understood early on they had to make things mistake-proof. This is the lesson to learn with designing any kind of system. If you can take out human error, you are going to be more successful." In the restaurant business, where customers are expecting their cheesy western or bowl of chile to be the same delicious way they like it every single time—whether it's at lunchtime or two o'clock in the morning—having fool-proof systems becomes supremely important. Matt found working at McDonald's fascinating. He never approached it as some throw-away fast food job. Rather, he looked at it as a learning opportunity.

"My dad always used to tell me, 'Listen, nobody's better than somebody else because of the type of job they do. Any job worth doing is worth doing well. Don't ever look down on anyone else for what they do for a living.'" Matt has recounted many of his father's personal wisdoms to me. He always states this one with particular fervor. Matt learned much from his six months working for the fast food chain and still counts it as one of his favorite jobs outside of his career.

For all the handy systems Matt learned from working at McDonald's, his most prized and personal Tavern system came not from the fast food chain, but from his father, and his father's father before him . . . and on and on. It's the little black notebook: a Bullington family system established at least five generations prior by Leander, who used it to record things like weather conditions and when he chopped wood. Matt swears by his small, pocket-sized, black spiral-bound notebook. Like his predecessors, Matt records each day's events however mundane they are. In this way, he has a continual reference tool for remembering anything from how he handled a similar employee situation to when he last spoke with the door framer about a job and what it was they'd discussed. It's seems fitting that Matt uses an archaic form of record keeping for the Tavern despite living in an era of advanced technology. That he uses the same system as his great-great-grandfather Leander—something he didn't realize until discovering it in one of his grandfather's boxes—is priceless.

✪ ✪ ✪ ✪ ✪ ✪ ✪ ✪ ✪ ✪ ✪ ✪ ✪ ✪

Matt's time with his dad to mentor him was more generous than either his father or grandfather had before him. Matt came into the family business full time in 1997, allowing Jim to enter into semiretirement. He and Velma bought a motor home and spent time traveling, eventually making it to every one of the lower forty-eight states. Jim also took up photography, learning it well enough to make it a retirement career. But when he wasn't traveling or snapping photos, Jim was present, imparting three decades of Tavern wisdom into his son. He'd also back up Matt so Matt could travel, first on his own, and eventually with his wife, Molly.

Molly and Matt Bullington.

Jim officially retired in 2005. At that time, Matt began buying the Texas Tavern. He also became its official owner and president. After retirement, Jim continued to make himself available. Matt even kept his office at his parent's house for years, using his dad's old office. He would go over to his parent's house once a week, do paperwork, then spend time and a meal with his folks and Molly, recounting to his dad the past week of Tavern's happenings. It wasn't until Matt and Molly started having children—Sam in 2009, Caroline in 2011—that he moved his office full time to his home.

"I feel very fortunate," said Matt to me in one of our last interviews. "I had the gift of having my dad as a mentor in a unique way. In life, yes. But also in my career."

Matt, his family, and Roanoke had the blessing of Jim Bullington until 2015. For several years, Jim's health had been in decline. In December of 2014, he was hospitalized for a lung infection complicated by emphysema. He never left the hospital. Jim passed away on Saturday, January 31, 2015. In Jim's seventy-six years of living, he spent thirty-eight of them stewarding the Tavern, fifty mentoring his children, and fifty-four loving his wife. As Velma expressed, "It was not quite long enough."

The lessons Matt gleaned from his father were countless. Sometimes the lessons were direct imperatives: *You have to know how to do everything better than anyone else*; or *Don't ever tell somebody to do something you're not willing to do*; or the one Matt deems most important: *Be fair. Always give people the benefit of the doubt. Always advocate for those less fortunate.*

Most of the time, however, Matt learned from his father through everyday conversations surrounding everyday situations. Something would come up—maybe with an employee, maybe with operations—and Matt would ask his dad, "Hey, [this thing] happened. What d'ya think?" Almost always, Jim's response would come in the form of a story, recounting a similar situation he'd faced—sometimes decades prior—and how he'd handled it. Matt appreciated his father's story-telling approach. Matt still remembers stories his dad shared with him from years ago. Over time, these storytelling conversations formed solid frameworks of indispensable wisdoms Matt still uses today. He will remember a story and hold his present situation up to it for illumination. It's problem-solving from a wise, generationally built perspective.

✪ ✪ ✪ ✪ ✪ ✪ ✪ ✪ ✪ ✪ ✪ ✪ ✪ ✪ ✪ ✪

When it comes to stewarding the ninety-year-old Texas Tavern, Matt finds navigating change one of his most challenging tasks. This includes changes in the culture as well as changes within the Tavern itself. When discussing this aspect of Tavern ownership, Matt often calls it a blessing and a curse.

"There is always a cost," explained Matt. "Not just a financial cost. There is a cost to making changes to the Tavern that fundamentally alter it. I am constantly balancing the questions out and asking myself, 'Will this [change] fundamentally alter the Tavern experience?'"

To be sure, for a business to remain viable, change must happen. Even if the business decides to stay the same and thrive, as the Bullingtons

Three generations of Bullingtons: Matt, his dad, Jim, and Sam, 2010. (Tina Holtzlander)

chose to do, microcosms of change still must occur. Matt admits that sometimes making changes at the Tavern can cause what he calls "analysis paralysis." He laughs when he says it, but he means it with all seriousness. While there are changes Matt can make without losing sleep, most decisions involving the Texas Tavern are heavily laden with consequence.

One way Matt tries to ease the pain of changing something of consequence is to spin it into a positive. This, too, Matt learned from his father. Back in 1988, when Jim decided it was time for the Tavern to transition from bottled sodas to a soda fountain, he turned it into a media opportunity. He did one of his classic shoulder-tappings to a member of the local press. The media did a short story on it. And Jim had his opportunity to publicly spin the change for the positive, helping Roanokers feel brought in and prepared for the epic transition. It probably helped that the Tavern kept bottled Cokes around for decades

The new, old Coca-Cola machine for bottled Cokes. (Molly Bullington)

afterwards. Not until 2000 did they finally decide to say goodbye to the bottled sodas altogether. But not forever.

While I was working on this book, Matt was facing one of these consequential, analysis/paralysis-type decisions. It involved the cigarette machine, a Tavern fixture since the 1960s. He wanted to get rid of the thing. In fact, he'd wanted to get rid of it for some time. He coveted the extra space he would gain by not having it. He really wanted to extend the narrow counter running along the back windows all the way to the end in order to increase the T.T.'s stand-up dining capacity. But the cigarette machine was decades old. To most Tavern customers, it was nearly as nostalgic as the quirky signs decorating the walls. Harry Connick Jr. even sang about the old cigarette machine in a funny ditty he made up during his last concert tour through Roanoke. It was one of those things that helped make the Tavern, *The Tavern*.

Or was it?

Matt labored over the decision. Nearly every time we met, he would bring it up. In a separate thread of conversations, he'd talk about his desire to bring back bottled Coca-Cola for special occasions. He was the one who brought back grape soda, something that had gone out during Jim's era of Tavern ownership.

Eventually, the two threads started weaving together. What if he could somehow make the removal of one thing an addition of something better? What if he removed the cigarette machine to make room for an old-fashioned bottled soda machine? He would still have more room than the cigarette machine allowed since the soda machine was smaller. He could still extend the back counter to the wall. He'd have a nifty way to bring back bottled Coca-Cola, along with a better way to store them, which was one reason they did away with bottled sodas to begin with. And if all this weren't smart enough, Matt would turn the entire changeover into a media opportunity.

"There's a legacy involved with the Tavern," Matt explained at one point during the cigarette-machine conundrum. "I take that pretty seriously."

✪ ✪ ✪ ✪ ✪ ✪ ✪ ✪ ✪ ✪ ✪ ✪ ✪ ✪ ✪

Texas Tavern may have a long legacy, but legacy is no granter of a secure tomorrow. The Bullingtons recognize their gift in owning the Tavern and its longevity. It is, after all, the oldest restaurant in all of Roanoke still operating in its original location. But Matt and Molly don't rest on their historic family laurels. The couple must work hard every single day, treating the Tavern like any other business. And just like any business, advertising is of primary concern.

One way the Bullingtons have kept up with changing cultural trends is by taking the Tavern "on the road," joining Roanoke's growing food-truck scene. In the summertime especially, Roanoke has become one giant festival. Nearly every weekend there is some event to attend, either downtown or in the surrounding neighborhoods. Matt created a Texas Tavern mobile setup with a trailer and shade tents. He and Molly started taking the Tavern to festivals in 2013. Early on, they did multiple events a season. However, as their kids have gotten older, the couple has become more particular about how many weekends they are willing to give up.

Matt also created the Texas Tavern's logo. It seems almost shocking to think the Tavern had existed for three generations without an official logo. And yet it wasn't until the bumper sticker craze hit that Matt felt he needed one. In 2010, he designed an official Texas Tavern logo, using the "EAT" sign as their guide. Matt sells the logo stickers for only a dollar apiece. They are wildly popular.

Both the Tavern logo and going mobile are perfect examples of something Matt is continually engaged in: grooming the next generation of Tavern goers. One of the things Matt often points to with regard to this new generation is the explosion of social media. While he shrugs off most online advertising, the Tavern does maintain a social media presence on Facebook, which Molly manages. Molly also handles much of the Tavern's photography—another important reality in today's media landscape. She credits both her father and father-in-law for her skill with the camera. Jim passed on his expertise and much of his equipment, while her father gifted her with his good eye for framing and design.

Beyond the advertising landscape, there is also the physical transformation of Roanoke's downtown spaces. What was once a bustling business and commerce center is now a tourist destination and restaurant mecca. There are more restaurants in downtown Roanoke than ever before in its history. The DowntownRoanoke.org website cites more than sixty. Matt is well aware of the cataclysmic shift in both advertising and the downtown-restaurant landscape. He refuses to let it distract him from his ultimate aim: caring for his customers.

"We don't worry about what other folks are doing competition-wise," said Matt. "The best advertising you can possibly do is make sure your customers are happy. Make sure your operations are sound and your employees are doing well." Matt always goes back to those very first lessons he learned from his father who, in turn, learned it from his father before him: always give the customer a fair shake, and make sure you're surrounded by good employees who are as committed to the customer as you are.

"I can figure out sourcing, pricing, and all the other things that are pretty simple in the grand scheme of things. There's so many moving parts, that's why it's important to have good employees. Nick understood this when he hired Van Cleve. My grandpa always had a heart for his employees. My dad understood it. He knew it was the most important part of running a business."

Without a doubt, Matt and Molly Bullington understand it, too.

A Perfect Beginning to Wedded Bliss

My husband, Taylor, and I got married at the Maridor on June 16, 2012. After a fun reception, we got in the car and headed to our honeymoon suite at the Hotel Roanoke. Taylor grew up in Virginia Beach and wasn't familiar with Roanoke. He nervously said to me, "Mandy, I didn't get anything to eat tonight and I'm starving. Would you mind if we went through a drive-thru on the way to the hotel?" I was raised in New Castle, Virginia, and grew up regularly visiting the Texas Tavern with my family. As soon as Taylor mentioned needing food, I thought about Texas Tavern. I tried to explain the T.T. to Taylor and finally just said, "Trust me."

We walked in wearing our wedding attire and immediately were welcomed by the employees and other guests. We took a seat and ordered our meal. Everyone was congratulating us and asking about our wedding day. Halfway through the meal, I remembered we couldn't pay with a credit card. I panicked. Neither of us had cash on us. I whispered to Taylor that he needed to run back to the car and open some of our wedding cards to find cash for our meal. As Taylor was getting up, a sweet couple walked up and put down a $20 bill. "Dinner is on us tonight," they said. "Keep the change. Congratulations!"

We had so much fun that evening and cherish the memory of our first meal as husband and wife at the Texas Tavern.

—Mandy Atkins, Roanoke

ON BEING
MRS. BULLINGTON

"I was just grateful. I was grateful he had the opportunity."

Velma Bullington
on her husband, Jim, taking over Tavern ownership.

"It's a really overwhelming feeling. . . .
We're a part of everyone's story. It's special."

Molly Bullington
on owning the Texas Tavern

"Gratitude, warm, sincere, intense, when it takes
possession of the bosom, fills the soul to overflowing and
scarce leaves room for any other sentiment or thought."

John Quincy Adams

✪ ✪ ✪ ✪ ✪ ✪ ✪ ✪ ✪ ✪ ✪ ✪ ✪ ✪ ✪ ✪

Early in my interview times with Matt, I recognized the serious role Bullington women have played in the success of the Texas Tavern. I met with Molly and Velma Bullington to hear what it's like being married, in essence, to the Texas Tavern.

"When I first met Jim, I was not into him at *all*," said Velma when telling her version of how they met. She recounted many of the same outward details as Jim's version. Except Velma's version sheds more light.

"I thought he was the cockiest guy I ever met!" she said, then laughed from the hilarity of it.

The truth is, Velma was interested in someone else that night she met Jim. She was seventeen years old, working at Fort Sam Houston, and taking night classes as she was able. She and Jim ended up at the same party by chance of having mutual connections. She danced with Jim once and barely remembered who he was when he called to ask her out a week later. The date didn't go well, culminating in Jim wanting them to split a hamburger at the drive-in theater and have her pay half. Velma thought he was full of himself and told him as much.

This might have scared off a different kind of man. But not Jim Bullington. He gave it time then called her and asked for a second date. Because she was bored and had nothing better to do, Velma agreed. This was a totally different Jim. After that date, Velma thought maybe Jim wasn't so cocky after all. Six months later, they were married. Velma was eighteen years old. Jim was twenty-one.

Molly and Matt's story also involved chance meetings and mutual connections. They ran in circles that overlapped other circles. But until the night they ended up at the same bar to watch the same band give its final performance, they'd never run in the same circle. Matt and Molly were both postcollegiate and working professionals when they met. Molly, a Charleston, South Carolina, native and graduate of Virginia Tech, was working in Roanoke with an engineering firm. Matt was already on his path to Tavern ownership. The couple dated five years before marrying.

"I finally told him I'd eat a bowl of chile when he proposed," said Molly, who doesn't care for beans of any kind, describing Matt's labored decision-making process. Then she and Velma both laughed at the striking difference between father and son.

"Matt's more like me that way," said Velma. "I'm more meticulous and careful. Not Jim. He'd just go with it, and if it was wrong, he'd change course along the way."

"And another good thing about Matt," added Molly, "is once he's made a decision he sticks with it and is good with it. He sees it through."

Each memory or observation begat another of the Texas Tavern and its men. One of Molly's favorite stories was of their weekly meals at Jim and Velma's and watching how Matt and Jim would chat about customers. Matt would tell his dad so-and-so came into the Tavern. Jim

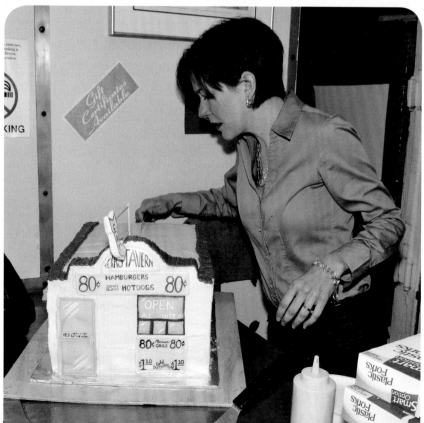

116

wouldn't know who Matt was talking about until Matt described the customer according to his or her dining habits.

"You know," Matt would say to his father, "two bowls with and a one with at 2 P.M."

"Oh, yeah!" Jim would say, and the conversation would continue.

Velma remembered the middle-of-the-night phone calls. There was the time they had just gotten to bed—it was right before Christmas and Jim and Velma had been up late putting toys together—when the phone rang. It was a Roanoke City police officer calling from the Tavern. The place was packed, the grill had hamburgers on it, and there was chile cooking on the back stove. But there were no employees. They'd all cut out and gone down to one of the bars on the Market. Jim had to rouse a neighbor. At two o'clock in the morning the two men drove down to the Tavern and kept it going through the night.

Throughout my time with Molly and Velma, two words kept floating across my mind: gratitude and joy. Velma grew up in San Antonio in a family "rich in love," as she described it, but that's about it. She'd worked from the time she was fourteen to help supplement the family income. Her father hunted for their food and taught Jim to do the same. She became good at cooking venison because that is what there was to eat. When Jim decided to take over the Tavern at a significant pay cut, they had two small children and one on the way. Velma had to keep the children quiet so Jim could sleep during the day.

I asked Velma what she was thinking during this time. "Well," she started, and then paused. "I was really grateful. I was grateful he had the opportunity."

Molly grew up steeped in a home where learning, Southern tradition, and history were highly esteemed. Business ownership and all the daunting tasks that come with it, such as self-promotion, for example, took some getting used to. Molly also feels the weight of responsibility

Opposite: Celebrating the 80th Anniversary of Texas Tavern are (above) Velma, Jim, and Sam and (below) Molly Bullington cutting the cake she made for the celebration.

she and Matt have toward their employees, customers, the community, and to the Tavern itself. Not to mention their family's livelihood.

When I asked Molly what she thinks of this life she married into, she said, "You know, it's like when you get married and you look at the room full of people and you realize they are all there for you. It's that overwhelming feeling that's similar to having the Tavern. We're a part of everyone's story. It's special."

T. T. and American Food Love

Since moving away from Roanoke, Texas Tavern has been the place I miss the most because of the excellent food and memories with my friends. As a foreigner [from South Korea], Texas Tavern provided unique American food I'd never experienced before. Chili became my most favorite American food, and no other chili has ever been better than a "bowl with." Once, I was given a gift certificate to Texas Tavern.

When I received the gift, I experienced a true dilemma: Was it better to keep the certificate and have a memento of Texas Tavern always with me? Or was it better to cash it in for another cheesy western? In the end, I couldn't resist eating another cheesy western.

—*Shawn Kim, Pensacola, Florida*

AFTER MIDNIGHT

"When the bars shut down, the Texas Tavern
gets to work sobering up the city."

Jim Bullington
third-generation Tavern owner

✪ ✪ ✪ ✪ ✪ ✪ ✪ ✪ ✪ ✪ ✪ ✪ ✪ ✪ ✪

If the Texas Tavern seems an anomaly during daytime hours, with its stripped-down menu, funny signs, and old-timey feel, after midnight it's a world unto itself.

The Tavern magically changes after midnight. No, they don't start taking credit cards—to the great dismay of many inebriated millennials looking for post-bar chow at 1 A.M. "What? You don't take credit cards?" they say with a sort of slur trying to snap itself into focus. Their eyes scan the place, then search the menu on the wall. They squint hard. Finally, they look back at the counterman and say, "Okay, well . . . uh . . . how about a cheeseburger with lettuce and tomatoes. Oh, and some fries."

Welcome to the Tavern after midnight.

I pulled one all-nighter at the Texas Tavern . . . almost. I worked from 10 P.M. to 2:30 A.M. on a late-July Saturday night. I knew I would never understand—nor be able to tell—the Tavern's story with any legitimacy if I didn't work the third shift on the weekend. I won't lie, I was full of equal parts concern, excitement, and dread. I had no idea what to expect. Would there be a mustard fight? A real fight? Another holdup? Would I be able to hang with the employees? Or just get in their way?

It turned out to be the perfect night for experiencing after hours at the Tavern. Downtown Roanoke was full of special events. There was a Radford University class reunion—some year from the early 1980s— being held a few blocks one direction from the Tavern. There was a Jerry Garcia tribute block party just around the corner on the other side. There was a concert at Elmwood Park. And there was all the usual nightlife happening in bars dotting the downtown.

the Roanoker

$1.00

WINTER
1978

WHERE TO EAT AFTER MIDNIGHT

FIRST ANNUAL DUBIOUS ACHIEVEMENT AWARDS

The Wacky Women At The Upper Cut

Why Industry Overlooks Roanoke

The Historic Elbert Waldron Home

**The Tragic Life And Death
Of Architect Robert Allen**

"After midnight" at the Tavern cover story for The Roanoker *magazine, 1978. (Courtesy* The Roanoker)

By the end of the night, the Tavern had welcomed them all.

The average age of each wave of folks was predictable—youngest to oldest, working back to young again. When I got to the Tavern at 10 P.M., there were several teenagers sitting at the counter eating their cheesys and drinking grape sodas. Chatting with them was natural, since they were the same ages as my own children. It was a blessed way to ease into the night. I hated to see them leave.

Shortly after the kids left, the third-shift crew—Cecil, the T.T.'s night manager; Chris; C. W.; and Cole—made plans for grill shifts. They split the shifts into one-hour blocks and matched grill experience to the projected busiest hours. Then they prepped their stations and readied the counter. They filled napkin containers, mustard bottles, salt and pepper, cracker packets, and stocked the grill station with all its essentials: buns, cheese, chile, hot dog chili, onions, pickles, Tavern relish, and any other thing needed for the onslaught of customers. The first big wave was the Radford reunion crew at 11:30 P.M. Most of these folks were first-timers, except for one woman, a local Roanoker, who was the reason they were all there. The woman kept trying to explain why they all *had* to experience the Tavern. Meanwhile, the friends stood against the back wall like confused tourists in a foreign country, staring at the menu and terrified to move. Finally, the woman started ordering. Some played along. Others couldn't get past the idea of chili at midnight in July.

While the Radford crew was still scratching their heads, I chatted with a couple from Smith Mountain Lake, a good forty-plus-minute drive from Roanoke, quietly satisfying their midnight cravings for Tavern chile and cheesys. An elderly couple also came in. Every once in a while, the husband looked my way, as though trying to adjust his eyes. Finally, he looked directly at me and said, "You know, I've been coming here since '61. My buddies and I used to cut out of school and come to the Tavern for lunch. In all my years, I've never seen a woman behind the counter."

With each wave, the customers grew younger and the interactions stranger. The 1:00 A.M. crowd was mostly Jerry Garcia folks. There were more first-timers and lots of conversations about not getting fries or paying with a credit card. The 2 A.M. wave—post-bar-goers—had a much better handle on their Tavern knowledge, and that was about it.

Through each wave, the guys behind the counter stayed steady and quick. C. W. multitasked like a pro: cooling beans, making batch after batch, and listening for the grill man to holler at him for food needs. Cecil was quick and steady on the grill: making cheesys and dipping bowls with while an open fire hose of orders kept coming at him. Cole tended to all the small details between customers. Chris became deliberate with his customer interactions. He'd stand directly in front of the customer, look the person in the eye, then repeat the order before calling it in.

It wasn't all serious behind the counter, however. Chris had fun cajoling customers with slivers of a hot pepper he'd brought to work. He'd suggest they add it to their cheesy westerns. More often than not, customers popped the pepper directly into their mouths, especially as the night wore on. That never got old.

Around 2:30 in the morning, a woman walked in, maneuvered herself through the crowd, and sat down at stool ten. She was fidgety and wore a wild look on her face. When I asked if she'd like a drink, she stared at me so hard I thought poison darts might shoot from her eyes. This, I decided, was my exit cue.

What a night. There were strange looks, high fives from customers, a few miscues, and even one or two smarmy remarks. All of it was worth missing a night of sleep. But there was one comment made by a regular customer I thought worth a whole month of third night shifts. It was around 1 A.M. The customer was on his second cheesy when he started waxing nostalgic with his friend.

"Think of it," the guy said. "We're looking at the exact same signs and same walls, eating at the exact same counter, sitting on the same stools. All of it's the same! This is what people were looking at in 1930! Crazy, man. So cool."

I couldn't agree more.

Like Grandmother, Like Granddaughter

I don't remember my first trip to the T.T. because I was just a little thing. I made so many trips with my Paw Paw, and as I got older, my friends and I would go for a late-night snack after being out on the town: "One cheesy, no pickle, bowl with, and a Diet Coke, please."

One night around the year 2000, when I was in my mid-twenties, I was sitting at the counter with my friend Leigh Ann. I was a little tipsy and she was our DD [designated driver] for the night. It was 1 A.M. and the place was pretty crowded. There was a wait for service, as it was two- and three-people deep. I started people watching and happened to spot someone in the crowd I knew. I whispered to Leigh Ann, in the loudest voice possible (remember the tipsy part): "You know your night is made when you spot your Grandma and her date in line behind you at the T.T.!"

Of course, the entire place heard me and laughed. I turned back around and ordered my grandma's food for her and then gave her our seats.

We still laugh about it to this day: seeing my almost seventy-year-old grandma, out after a night of karaoke, and us twenty-something's bar hopping, all at the T.T. for cheesy westerns.

—Denise Hodges, Roanoke

TAVERN TIME

"Time present and time past
Are both perhaps present in time future,
And time future contained in time past."
7. S. Eliot
"Burnt Norton"

"For everything there is a season,
and a time for every matter under heaven."
Ecclesiastes 3:1

✪ ✪ ✪ ✪ ✪ ✪ ✪ ✪ ✪ ✪ ✪ ✪ ✪ ✪ ✪ ✪ ✪

Our culture talks and complains so much about the speed of life, it has nearly become cliché. We fly through the hours of our days, never feeling comfortable with the pace we keep. Yet we have no idea what to do with ourselves when we actually have a period of time not crammed with meetings, appointments, kid events . . .on and on. Add to this the extreme pressures of our late-modern society to achieve all things, be all things, know all things, obtain all things. No wonder we see time as this hateful enemy, stealing from us and leaving us helpless, half-finished human beings.

But to walk into the Tavern is to step into the past and leave linear time behind. It's resting one's feet upon the metal foot railing worn through from generations of feet rubbing against it. It's eating at the same dented silver counter folks ate at ninety years ago. It's being surrounded by the same decor, same pithy signs, and nearly the same menu. All these markers from the past provide a sort of rest for the weary, linear-time-worn soul. Sure, the food is still prepared fast, and sometimes the ten stools are taken and you have to wait your turn. But even these time-sensitive realities are the same as they were in 1930, and

Inside the timeless Texas Tavern, ca. 1934.

will be the same twenty years from now. If anything, these aspects of time spent in the Tavern add to the overall feeling of stepping out of the rat race and into another more generous dimension.

This is where the real magic of the Texas Tavern begins. By connecting ourselves with a bygone era, we do more than step away from the chaos of our days. We awaken something within us, reminding us that we are more than hamsters in a wheel. We are woven through with the ability to imagine the future and have memories of the past. We can have dreams and recollections. We can think ahead and learn from what we've done. When we ignore this, we lose our nature, even our very souls. We become less human. But to step into Tavern Time is to enliven our souls while simultaneously feeding our stomachs.

Maybe it's a stretch, this idea of eating a cheesy western or bowl of chile and actually growing in wholeness as a person, too. Maybe it's even absurd. Or maybe it's another gift offered us through the Tavern's story: the generous spirit found only in Tavern Time.

"Just like chili on a hot dog"

The Texas Tavern is and has always been my favorite restaurant. A very special person introduced it to me about twenty-five years ago. My father first went when he moved to Roanoke in 1973 and took his first two sons there around the mid-80s. In the early 1990s, it was my turn.

Being young, I was an incredibly picky eater. I got what they called "streakers," just a plain hotdog—no bun, no nothing. Gradually, I worked my way to a bun and had plain hots.

Soon, I branched out and tried some of the other "T'n'T" menu items. I loved the burgers, the chile, and even cheesy westerns. But I was always reticent on trying the hotdog chili. Any time Dad and I went and I got plain hots, he'd ask: "Why don't you get chili on those? It's phenomenal and you'll love it. You won't have them any other way once you try 'em."

One day, I acquiesced and got a "hot with"—no onions, no relish. Took one bite and to my utter amazement, it changed my life. . . . My dad was totally right.

After that experience, whenever I was reticent about trying something new . . . [my dad would] say: "It's like the chili on the hotdog."

It was like pulling teeth, but my Dad got me out of my comfort zone by bringing me to the Texas Tavern. It was that small lesson that opened up so many other doors and opportunities in life, and I have him to thank for it.

—Christian Gold
in tribute to his father, Dr. Walter Gold,
who passed away May 27, 2019. "Best Friend, Mentor, Confidant"

CLOSING
THOUGHTS

✪ ✪ ✪ ✪ ✪ ✪ ✪ ✪ ✪ ✪ ✪ ✪ ✪ ✪

I began my journey into writing this book with several questions: What makes a restaurant more than a restaurant? What makes a burger, chile, and hot dog joint a cultural mooring? And how is the South's unique relationship with food particularly situated to best answer these questions?

There is an old Native American proverb that says: "Tell me a fact and I'll learn. Tell me the truth and I'll believe. But tell me a story and it will live in my heart forever." The essence and lasting impact of any culture can often be found in the power of its stories.

Food, says the Southerner, is story. The Three Sisters—beans, corn, and squash—tell the story of the Native Americans and their influence on early colonists to Southern Appalachia. Okra, varieties of yams, sorghum, and watermelon (among other foods) tell the story of the West African people and the tragic reality of slave trade. Dishes like Hoppin' John, gumbo, goulash, and cornbread tell stories of the resiliency of people in the face of adversity and suffering. They also tell the story of the hard, uneven, and ongoing work of reconciliation.

The Texas Tavern is a cultural mooring because it is a Southern food story. It's four generations of one family choosing to steward their life and community through food. The Tavern is steeped in the specifics of its time and place while simultaneously transcending time by its very expression and dedication to its place. Through its story, the Tavern reveals eternal truths and lights a good way forward. Finally, because the Tavern is a food story, it culminates in communion. It's the communion of high society and homeless, of blue blood and blue collar.

And the substance of their communion? Hamburgers, hot dogs, cheesy westerns, and chile, prepared with integrity, served with humility, eaten with thanksgiving.

This is the power of ten bar stools at a dented stainless counter in a ninety-year-old diner. This is the Texas Tavern, four generations of the Millionaires Club.

Acknowledgments

When I accepted the project of writing the Texas Tavern's story, I was terrified. I couldn't fathom how I ended up with this task so high in honor and deep in responsibility. Still, I shake my head when thinking of it. Only by the support of the community surrounding me has this book come to fruition.

I want to thank the entire Bullington family for putting their trust in me. They didn't know me when we began this project. They opened their personal lives and entrusted me with their most sacred possession: their family's generational story and legacy. Thank you to Matt, with whom I spent most of my time, for sitting hours on end answering questions, recalling stories, pulling photographs, and allowing me special access to the Tavern. Thank you to Molly, who helped gather photography and customers' stories, shared her life, and befriended me. Thank you to Velma, who welcomed me as a daughter and not an outsider and who breathed life into the Tavern's story in ways only a wife and mother can do.

I want to extend my hearty thanks to all the Texas Tavern employees. They put up with me for hours at a time, invading their tiny workspace. I know I was often in the way, but they never let on. They were always kind, gentlemanly, and charitable in answering my questions and letting me "help" behind the counter. Thanks also to David Bullington and Nelson Harris for taking time out of their days, helping me understand Roanoke's history and how the Bullingtons' story is woven through it.

I am forever thankful to Kurt Rheinheimer, senior editor at Leisure Media 360. When Fred Sauceman, the series editor for *Food and the American South*, asked him what local writer would do well telling the Tavern's story, Kurt thought of me. Anytime I felt unqualified or bogged down by the enormity of the project, I would remind myself,

"Kurt believes I can do this." We should all be so fortunate to have a "Kurt" in our vocational lives.

Thank you to all the folks connected with Mercer University Press. I am especailly indebted to Fred Sauceman, Dr. Marc Jolley, and Marsha Luttrell. Their enthusiasm and constant support put my mind at ease more times than they could ever know. They, too, have bolstered my confidence in the work and made this project a joy.

To my husband, Tony, who believed in writing as my vocation before I did, thank you. Also, thanks for telling me I was crazy if I didn't accept this project, for sending me away so I could write, and for doing "all the things" at home during deadline month.

If there is anything of value that I've contributed in telling the Texas Tavern's story, it has come from the way I was raised. By their everyday example, my parents taught me true beauty is cultivated when food, place, and people come together in a shared experience. They also taught me it's my responsibility to be a cultivator. Thank you, Mom and Dad.